# THE AMERICAN REVOLUTION

## IN THE

# TWENTY-FIRST CENTURY

*Howard DeLong*

A revised and retitled version of
*Common Reason and Uncommon Politics:*
*The American Revolution in the Twenty-First Century*
Copyright © 2019 by Howard DeLong


DeLong, Howard
The American Revolution
in the Twenty-First Century/Howard DeLong
116 pages: 23 cm

ISBN 978-0-578-72427-0


1. United States — The Revolution, 1775-1783 — General special
2. United States — The Revolution, 1775-1783 — Political history
3. United States — Politics and government — Philosophy
E209 .D45 2021


BELCREST PRESS
WEST HARTFORD, CT

THE GREATEST GIFT WE COULD GIVE OUR
CHILDREN IS A TWENTY-FIRST CENTURY AMERICAN
REVOLUTION THAT WOULD  INSTILL IN THEM THE
ETHICAL AND ASPIRATIONAL VIRTUES NEEDED TO
PRODUCE EXCELLENCE IN GOVERNMENT AND
FLOURISHING LIVES FOR THEMSELVES.

# PREFACE

**George Mason:** "That no free Government, or the blessings of liberty, can be preserved to any people but by . . . frequent recurrence to fundamental principles."

**James Wilson:** "There is not in the whole science of politicks a more solid or a more important maxim than this—that of all governments, those are the best, which, by the natural effect of their constitutions, are frequently renewed or drawn back to their first principles."

The history of the American Revolution is well known, but its philosophy is hardly known at all. Our political leaders have therefore been oblivious to their awesome responsibility to take a giant step toward furthering that revolution. That step will be as challenging as the first step was for the generation of 1776. If taken, it could create a new and transcendent form of democracy that promises to solve political problems that are at present unsolvable.

To give authoritative voice to this philosophy, I have quoted liberally from eighteenth-century Americans expressing it, setting off in bold type (as above), the names of the authors. This allows readers to experience directly the enormous excitement that its philosophy had on the generation of 1776. (All other quotations are not so highlighted.) For them, the American Revolution was understood as not only political, but as creating a new kind of consciousness, a new kind of civilization that would allow all Americans to prosper in their pursuit of happiness. This book depicts the intellectual, moral, and political challenges that we must solve to live up to those aspirations. The philosophy of the American Revolution is moribund, but we have the responsibility to give it a rebirth, and to embody its practice with an unprecedented degree of excellence in the cause of humanity.

## PERFECTIONIST ASPIRATIONS

When so many citizens consider our politics a great embarrassment, with consequent worries that reach to the existential, it is well past time to recur to America's founding philosophy. There we are perhaps astounded to find, among realistic political leaders, widespread expression of perfectionist aspirations for the American people and their politics. Listen to the first four presidents:

**George Washington:** In 1783 Washington closed his address to the army officers with these words: "You will, by the dignity of your Conduct, afford occasion for Posterity to say, when speaking of the glorious example you have exhibited to Mankind, 'had this day been wanting, the World had never seen the last stage of perfection to which human nature is capable of attaining.' "

**John Adams:** "We are in the very midst [June 9,1776] of a Revolution, the most compleat, unexpected, and remarkable of any in the History of Nations. . . . Every Colony must be induced to institute a perfect Government."

**Thomas Jefferson:** "I am among those who think well of the human character generally. I consider man as formed for society, and endowed by nature with those dispositions which fit him for society. I believe also . . . that his mind is perfectible to a degree of which we cannot as yet form any conception."

**James Madison:** Our "common Government . . . if supported by wise councils, by virtuous conduct, & by mutual & friendly allowances, must approach as near to perfection as any human work can aspire."

Today such perfectionist respect for humanity and its politics is virtually never expressed; to our cynical age it reflects an optimism about human nature that appears both dangerously naive and utterly baffling. Nevertheless, that respect did not result in a pernicious utopianism, illustrated by Plato, Marx, Hitler, Al-Qaeda, the Taliban, or ISIS. These men or organizations recommended, or carried out, political manipulation, or lies, or repression, or torture, or murder, or mass terror to further their aims, or to silence criticism of their views. Thus the fanatical perfectionism of Osama bin Laden is revealed in *The Al-Qaeda Training Manual*: "The confrontation that we are calling for with the apostate regimes does not know Socratic debates, Platonic ideals, nor Aristotelian diplomacy. But it knows the dialogue of bullets, the ideals of assassination, bombing and destruction, and the diplomacy of the cannon and machine-gun." American perfectionism is the radical antithesis of such utopianism because it is peaceful, empirical, and guarantees the right of criticism, including democratic revision in light of those criticisms. Its theory requires self-evidence and then proof, as in Euclidean geometry.

**Alexander Hamilton:** "In disquisitions of every kind there are certain primary truths, or first principles, upon which all subsequent reasonings must depend. . . . Of this nature are the maxims in geometry, that 'The whole is greater than its part; . . . that all right angles are equal to each other.' Of the same nature are these other maxims in ethics and politics, that there cannot be an effect without a cause; that the means ought to be proportioned to the end."

In Euclidean geometry, "all right angles are equal to each other"; in the Declaration of Independence, "all Men are created equal." Each is axiomatic and held to be self-evident, neither is given a proof, and both are perfectionist. Valid proofs, from the self-evident axioms of either geometry or politics, must, in principle, justify all subsequent theorems.

Turning from theory to practice requires careful observation, experiment, and demonstration, as in Newtonian science. The mathematical elegance and empirical success of Newton's theory of planetary motion were used to illustrate hopes for a politics that was similarly perfectionist *and* experimental:

**Thomas Jefferson:** "I dare say that in time all these [state governments] as well as their central government, like the planets revolving round their common Sun, acting & acted upon according to their respective weights & distances, will produce that beautiful equilibrium on which our constitution is founded, and which I believe it will exhibit to the world in a degree of perfection unexampled but in the planetary system itself."

**James Wilson:** "The immortal Newton collected, arranged, and formed his just and beautiful system of experimental philosophy. By the same kind of process, our predecessors and ancestors have collected, arranged, and formed a system of experimental law, equally just, equally beautiful, and, important as Newton's system is, far more important still."

In the beauty of aesthetic ideals, Euclidean geometry, Newtonian physics, and American politics were born. But politicians today are not aesthetically inspired by our best contemporary mathematics and science. For instance, in 1919 Hendrik Lorentz said Einstein's general theory of relativity "has the very highest degree of aesthetic merit: every lover of the beautiful must wish it to be true." In 1932 Ernest Rutherford said: "The [general] theory of relativity by Einstein, quite apart from any question of its validity, cannot but be regarded as a magnificent work of art." Our contemporary political or economic proposals should meet this standard, but they seldom, if ever, do. What proposals, like general relativity, are both valid and "a magnificent work of art"? In the commercial world Steve Jobs understood, as many of his competitors did not, that *humans are aesthetic animals*. He added incredible wealth to the American economy, and achieved lasting fame, through "magical" products that were not created by magic, but by aesthetic aspiration and engineering excellence. The Founders wanted "magical" governments—"as near to perfection as any human work can aspire"—to provide the conditions for citizens to reach the highest degree of excellence in the art of living of which they were capable, an art they called the pursuit of happiness. Unfortunately, their laws did not come close to approximating their own aesthetic standard.

## UGLY LAWS

**James Madison:** "It will be of little avail to the people, that the laws are made by men of their own choice, if the laws be so voluminous that they cannot be read, or so incoherent that they cannot be understood; if they be repealed or revised before they are promulgated, or undergo such incessant changes that no man who knows what the law is to-day can guess what it will be to-morrow. . . Another effect of public instability is the unreasonable advantage it gives to the sagacious, the enterprising and the moneyed few, over the industrious and uninformed mass of the people. Every new regulation concerning commerce or revenue, or in any manner affecting the value of the different species of property, presents a new harvest to those who watch the change, and can trace its consequences; a harvest, reared not by themselves, but by the toils and cares of the great body of their fellow-citizens."

It would be hard to top Madison's words for a succinct criticism of Congress as it has actually developed. The vices of which he speaks have grown exponentially. The aspiration for rule by the people has resulted in an oligarchic republic, not a democratic one. Rule-by-the-few trumped rule-by-the-many. Consider an "incoherent" passage from the Medicare law that only "the sagacious, the enterprising and the moneyed few" have the resources to interpret: "In the case of a plan for which there are average per capita monthly savings described in section 1395w-24(b)(3)(C) or 1395w-24(b)(4)(C) of this title, as the case may be, the amount specified in this subparagraph is equal to the unadjusted MA statutory non-drug monthly bid amount, adjusted under subparagraph (C) and (if applicable) under subparagraphs (F) and (G), plus the amount (if any) of any rebate under subparagraph (E)."

Every lover of the beautiful must loathe the ugliness that is embodied in our laws, but our legislators think ugliness is perfectly appropriate for the people they represent. Dead in their consciousness is the revolutionary ideal that the entire legal code should accurately reflect the common reason of the people, and be expressed in a language that is everywhere a masterpiece of precision, simplicity, beauty, and perspicuity. Instead Congress has produced a vast aesthetic wasteland of disfigured laws written in the Kafkaesque language of unintelligibility, designed to protect special interest law from public scrutiny. Such ugliness contradicts the philosophy of the American Revolution which aspires to governments that "will exhibit to the world in a degree of perfection, unexampled but in the planetary system itself." The effect of these governments, like Job's iPhones, would be "magical," though also not created by magic, but by aesthetic aspiration and engineering excellence.

John Adams rightly called himself the "principal Engineer" of the Massachusetts Constitution (1780). In a conceptual sense, that Constitution was one of the grand staircases that led up to the civic acropolis of American politics—the Declaration, the Constitution, the Bill of Rights—each a triumph of eighteenth-century aesthetic engineering. Civic engineers responsible for the creation of constitutions, like civil engineers responsible for the creation of grand public buildings or monuments, should be masters at expressing the spirit of the people, a task that requires meticulous preparation, careful observation, controlled experiment, technological prowess and monumental, even awesome, artistry. (There should not be a pejorative use of *social engineer*, since it reflects a misunderstanding of engineering; the correct pejorative phrase is *social dabblers*.) American revolutionists thought of themselves as unique because they had the opportunity, without using force or fraud, to engineer beautifully designed governments embodying equality, liberty, and justice.

## AMERICA'S TRAGIC FLAW

Having been asked why "all free persons of a black Complexion" could not vote, Lieutenant Governor William Gooch of Virginia answered in 1735 that the "Assembly thought it necessary . . . to fix a perpetual Brand upon Free-Negros & Mulattos by excluding them from that great Priviledge of a Freeman . . . And 'tis likewise said to have been done with design, which I must think a good one, to make the free-Negros sensible that a distinction ought to be made between their offspring and the Descendants of an

Englishman, with whom they never were to be Accounted Equal."
After the revolution, the attempt to construct actual governments
based on strongly anti-utopian, but perfectionist aspirations tied to
experiment, led to a federal system that was glorious in many
respects. Nevertheless, under that system the monstrous institution
of slavery based on color, which is despicable in every way, was
continued and greatly strengthened in spite of a large eighteenth-
century literature against these injustices that were clearly contrary to
the principles of the revolution. Here are a few samples:

**Andrew Eliot (1774):** "The meanest slave hath a soul as
good by nature as your's, and possibly by grace it is better . A dark
complection may cover a fair and beautiful mind. Every soul is
beautiful, that resembles the moral character of the blessed God, who
is the standard of perfection."

**"The petition of A Great Number of Blackes detained
in a State of slavery"(1777):** "Every Principle from which
Amarica has Acted in the Cours of their unhappy Deficultes with
Great Briton Pleads Stronger than A thousand arguments in favowrs
of your petioners."

**David Cooper (1783):** Cooper quoted from the Declaration
of Independence and said: "We need not now turn over the libraries
of Europe for authorities to prove that blacks are born equally free
with whites; it is declared and recorded as the sense of America."

**"Republicus"(1788):** 'Tell us, ye who can thus, cooly,
reduce the impious principle of slavery, to a constitutional system: ye
professed violators of liberties of mankind: where will ye stop? what
security can you give, that, when there shall remain no more black
people, ye will not enslave others, white as yourselves? when Africa
is exhausted, will ye spare America?'" (Notice that this is the same

type argument Ruth Bader Ginsburg used in showing that the laws that are used against women can be used against men.)

**William Pinkney (1789):** From a speech in the House of Delegates of Maryland: "It will not do . . . to talk like philosophers, and act like unrelenting tyrants; to be perpetually sermonizing it with liberty for our text, and actual oppression for our commentary . . . these shackled wretches are men as well as we are, sprung from the same common parent, and endued with equal faculties of mind and body. . . . Born with hearts as susceptible of virtuous impressions as our own, and with minds as capable of benefiting by improvement, they are in all respects our equals by nature."

**Abraham Bishop (1791):** "I speak the words of truth and soberness, in saying, that the blacks are now fighting in a just cause.My assertion, that they are entitled to freedom, is founded on the American Declaration of Independence. . . . for we did not say, all *white* men are *free*, but *all men* are free." "The blacks are still enslaved within the United States. The Indians are driven into the society of savage beasts, and we glory in the equal rights of men, provided that *we white men can enjoy the whole of them.*"

**George Buchanan (1793):** "To the eternal infamy of our country [slavery] will be handed down to posterity, written with the blood of African innocence."

And so it happened. The Founders were men of high integrity in many respects, but for most of them that integrity did not include the subjects of blacks or slavery. For example, Patrick Henry explicitly acknowledged his weakness of will and continuing hypocrisy: "I am drawn along by [the] general inconvenience of living without them; I will not, I cannot justify it. However culpable my Conduct, I will so far pay my devoir to Virtue, as to own the excellence & rectitude of her Precepts, & to lament my want of conforming to them." Henry even used the image of the slave with great rhetorical effect in his celebrated "Give Me Liberty or Give Me Death" speech. An eyewitness reports: "When he said, 'Is life so dear, or peace so sweet, as to be purchased at the price of chains and slavery?' he stood in the attitude of a condemned galley slave, loaded with fetters, awaiting his doom. His form was bowed; his wrists were crossed; his manacles were almost visible as he stood like an embodiment of helplessness and agony. After a solemn pause, he raised his eyes and chained hands towards heaven, and prayed, in words and tones which thrilled every heart, 'Forbid it, Almighty God!'." One wonders if Henry ever recognized a kindred spirit when he heard of a slave either escaping to freedom, or dying in the attempt. The wonder ceases, however, when one learns that neither while living nor in his will did Henry ever free a slave, and that "They'll free your niggers!" are words he used in arguing against ratification of the Constitution.

Bad as it is, Henry's type of hypocrisy is not the worst corruption of mental life. The worst is a type of self-deception. With regard to slavery, it existed in the minds of many revolutionary leaders, but perhaps none possessed a higher degree of it than Jefferson. The glorious Declaration of American Independence was composed by him and, as he later rightly claimed, its authority depended "on the harmonizing sentiments of the day." Yet within five years he was composing his *Notes on the State of Virginia,* which contained what deserves to be called the Declaration of American Racism, whose authority rested on divisive prejudices of the day; prejudices that Jefferson was the first American—perhaps even the first human being—to collect, summarize, and express publicly. The same talent that produced the magnificent concision in the cause of humanity in his first Declaration was then used in the second Declaration in the cause of inhumanity.

In the latter Declaration, he claimed that color *is* important; that blacks are not as beautiful as whites; that they have an inferior form and hair; that the male "Oran-ootan" prefers black women to females of its own kind; that blacks give off "a very strong and disagreeable odour"; that "their griefs are transient"; that their imagination is "dull, tasteless, and anomalous"; that he could not find a black who had "uttered a thought above the level of plain narration"; that blacks are incapable of poetry and geometry; that the "improvement of the blacks in body and mind, in the first instance of their mixture with the whites, has been observed by every one, and proves that their inferiority is not the effect merely of their condition of life." If this claimed *proof* in his racist Declaration is true, the Declaration of Independence is false. Such was Jefferson's monstrous self-delusion that this gross contradiction was apparently unknown to him, he believed both Declarations, he was somehow smart enough to fool himself.

But many others were not fooled. During his lifetime his racist views were criticized by David Ramsay, Gilbert Imlay, Duc de La Rochefoucauld-Liancourt, Edward Rushton, William Linn, Oliver Oldschool (pseudonym), Samuel Smith, and Clement Clarke Moore of *The Night Before Christmas* fame. Moore owned slaves and didn't disapprove of slavery. Yet he says: "Among the numerous opportunities which Mr. Jefferson must have had of observing the dispositions of these unfortunate people, did he never discover in any instance a nobleness of spirit, and delicate sense of honour, not exceeded by any hero of history or romance? Or did he always see through the fallacious medium of a darling theory?"

In 1791 Jefferson received a letter from Benjamin Banneker, who described himself as "of the African race, and in that colour which is natural to them of the deepest dye." He enclosed an almanac he had written that demonstrated sophisticated ability in geometry. Characteristically, Jefferson attacks the evidence. He writes to Joel Barlow: "We know he had spherical trigonometry enough to make almanacs, but not without the suspicion of aid from Ellicot, who was his [white] neighbor & friend, & never missed an opportunity of puffing him. I have a long letter from Banneker which shews him to have had a mind of very common stature indeed." Jefferson deprecates Banneker's talents because the existence of even one mathematically talented, pure African contradicted his "proof" that the black race is, by nature, inferior.

**Benjamin Banneker:** "This, Sir, was a time [1776] in which you clearly saw into the injustice of a State of Slavery, and in which you had just apprehensions of the horrors of its condition, it was now Sir, that your abhorrence thereof was so excited, that you publickly held forth this true and invaluable doctrine, which is worthy to be recorded and remember'd in all Succeeding ages: 'We hold these truths to be Self evident, that all men are created equal, and that they are endowed by their creator with certain unalienable rights, that among these are life, liberty, and the pursuit of happiness.' Here, Sir, was a time in which your tender feelings for your selves had engaged you thus to declare, you were then impressed with proper ideas of the great valuation of liberty, and the free possession of those blessings to which you were entitled by nature, but Sir how pitiable is it to reflect, that altho you were so fully convinced of the benevolence of the Father of mankind, and of his equal and impartial distribution of those rights and privileges which he had conferred upon them, that you should at the Same time counteract his mercies, in detaining by fraud and violence so numerous a part of my brethren under groaning captivity and cruel oppression, that you should at the Same time be found guilty of that most criminal act, which you professedly detested in others, with respect to yourselves."

Although Banneker's letter is a paradigm of speaking truth to power, Jefferson's "darling theory" prevents him from seeing the truth. "Few love to hear the sins they love to act"(Shakespeare). Again, during Jefferson's lifetime, George Buchanan, John Gabriel Stedman, Voltaire, Thomas Branagan, Thomas Clarkson, Johann Blumenbach, Gilbert Imlay, Benjamin Rush, Henri Grégoire, Samuel Stanhope Smith, and George Washington could praise the work of Phillis Wheatley, a black poet. What does Jefferson say? "The compositions published under her name are below the dignity of criticism." "It will be right to make great allowances for the difference of condition, of education, of conversation, of the sphere in which [blacks] move." Yet when Jefferson comes up against evidence contrary to his "darling theory" of racism, he makes no "allowances," but instead introduces doubts about the evidence itself. About Banneker, he has "suspicion of aid from Ellicott"; about Ignatius Sancho, he raises doubts that Sancho's letters are "genuine," or at least unamended by whites; he refers to Wheatley's work as "compositions published under her name"; and his reply to Banneker includes this gross self-deceit in evaluating his own probity: "No body wishes more than I do to see such proofs as you exhibit, that nature has given to our black brethren, talents equal to those of the other colours of men." This is an ugly, but common, example of the powerful speaking false to the politically powerless.

**Thomas Paine:** "It is impossible to calculate the moral mischief, if I may so express it, that mental lying has produced in society. When a man has so far corrupted and prostituted the chastity of his mind, as to subscribe his professional belief to things he does not believe he has prepared himself for the commission of every other crime."

One of those crimes from self-deception, in Jefferson's case, was torture. In 1805 Jame Hubbard escaped from Monticello, but was captured. In 1810 he escaped again and was brought back in chains. As Jefferson describes his own cruel crime, "I had him severely flogged in the presence of his old companions, and committed to jail." This is but one of many things that Jefferson "handed down to posterity, written with the blood of African innocence." From Great Britain, Thomas Day's 1776 observation seems especially relevant: "If there be an object truly ridiculous in Nature, it is an American patriot signing resolutions of independency with the one hand, and with the other brandishing a whip over his affrighted slaves." Of course, Jefferson's "professional belief" was revealed when he composed, not merely just signed, a resolution of independency asserting "unalienable Rights" for all humans.

In his authoritative *Commentaries on the Laws of England* (1765-1769), William Blackstone says that the creator "graciously reduced the rule of obedience to this one paternal precept, 'that man should pursue his own happiness.' This is the foundation of what we call ethics, or natural law. ... This law of nature, being co-eval with mankind and dictated by God himself, is of course superior in obligation to any other. It is binding over all the globe, in all countries, and at all times: no human laws are of any validity, if contrary to this." The slave laws of Virginia and the petty slave laws of Monticello had no validity since they were contrary to the natural law ethics of the Declaration of Independence.

So why did Jefferson not use his superb intellect and unmatched literary talent to propose reasonable means for ending the institution of slavery? Why did he not do scores of things that someone of his imagination, gifts, and power could easily conceive? The answer is that to take such a course, he would first have had to admit to himself the enormously painful idea that, by the ethical and political standards for whose articulation he was justly famous, and to which he had pledged his life, his fortune, and his sacred honor, by those standards he had been a tyrant and a depraved man; and that the Virginia society that he loved, and the lavish Monticello lifestyle that he enjoyed, were founded on a moral abomination. They each richly deserved a revolution—if necessary, a violent one—by the principles that he so magnificently expressed. To live with himself Jefferson chooses, not honest self-evaluation, but a self-delusion that makes the moral rot in his soul invisible to his mind's eye.

**John Cooper (1780):** "If we are determined not to emancipate our slaves, but to hold them still in bondage, let us alter our language upon the subject of tyranny; let us no longer speak of it as a thing in its own nature detestable, because in so doing . . . we shall condemn ourselves. But let us rather declare to the world, that tyranny is a thing we are not principled against, but that we are resolved not to be slaves, because we ourselves mean to be tyrants."

I think Jefferson forces every patriot of the Declaration of Independence into an uncomfortable, even tormenting, ambivalence; Dr. Jekyll-Jefferson's immense contributions to the American Revolution must continue to inspire awe and enormous gratitude; yet

Mr. Hyde-Jefferson's betrayal of that revolution by his treachery toward blacks destroys any respect for his moral character. It requires relentless condemnation from every friend of humanity. The awesome powers of critical thinking that Jefferson possessed were utterly worthless to protect him from great disgrace in our eyes, because he depraved his own consciousness, rendering impotent those awesome powers where they were most needed. He could not think like Cooper to understand himself, he was no mind reader of his own mind. Jefferson's gross moral cowardice completely annihilates the capacity for *self-critical* thinking, a destruction that allows him to become a natural law criminal with a clear conscience. Sometimes good reasoning requires good character.

Jefferson not only harbored an irrational Negrophobia himself; his literary and political talent enabled him to become a highly successful entrepreneur in selling his self-delusion, his racist "darling theory," to others. Jefferson did not invent racism, but he became the greatest contributor to corrupting the public mind by transmitting his own racist consciousness into it. Since human minds that are incapable of honest self-evaluation can be the greatest of all weapons of mass destruction—"When I think about it," Hitler once said, "I realize that I'm extraordinarily humane."—we cannot start too early, or be too careful, or be too persistent, in protecting ourselves and our country against such abominations.

## COURTS OF COMMON REASON

Slavery continued in America, followed by peonage and Jim Crow beyond that, because *elective representative democracy* has a gross systemic weakness—namely, the infidelity by political leaders to the public good. This weakness is caused by ignorance of that good, or the proper means to achieve it, or by motives contrary to it, which, if they be known to the politician we call *hypocrisy*; if unknown, *self-deceit*. So why should we keep our representative political system that nearly had an existential failure in abolishing slavery? Or keep it after it took a century more to get rid of peonage and Jim Crow, and even then without solving major racial troubles? Or keep it currently when party squabbles, flawed laws, embarrassing and incompetent leaders, widespread corruption, and frequent legislative gridlock seem to portend America's permanent decline, and eventually its existence? Incredibly, our eighteenth-century ancestors thought of something better than elective representative democracy. Let us listen *and* learn from them.

**Thomas Jefferson:** Jefferson wanted the body politic of Virginia broken down into small political units he called *wards*. There "the voice of the whole people would be . . . fairly, fully, and peaceably expressed, discussed, and decided by the common reason of the society." Wards "will be pure and elementary republics, the sum of all which, taken together, compose the State." Dividing Virginia into wards would enable the people "to crush, regularly and peaceably, the usurpations of their unfaithful agents, and rescues them from the dreadful necessity of doing it insurrectionally."

If the *common reason of the people* is the ultimate criterion that decides whether or not there are any "usurpations of their unfaithful agents," it takes no prodigious intellectual effort to conclude validly that our political leaders have no honorable choice; they have to authorize institutions that will accurately articulate that reason. We rightly denounce the Founders for having liberty, liberty, liberty on their lips, and then doing little to eradicate slavery.

The same kind of hypocrisy and self-deceit applies to our leaders, who have the people, the people, the people on their lips, but who then treat them as incapable of common reason, as only worthy of manipulation.

What should our leaders be doing to rid us of the evils of elective representative democracy?  We can begin to answer that question by conducting a thought experiment in which we assume an *Agency for Common Reason* is formed à la NASA.  Its task will be called *Project Athena* which, à la Project Apollo, will have a ten-year goal for completion.  Its aim is to identify precisely, efficiently, and routinely, the common reason of the American people on any political issue.  Project Athena would radically transform our governments by giving the ultimate supremacy to the people, but *not* to their whims, casual opinions, or prejudices.  For the first time in its history, the United States would have "magical" governments—dare I say perfect governments?—that do nothing contrary to the public good. The people, in a deliberative frame of mind, operationally *define* the public good, and they collectively have no motive to ever act against it.  American history is filled with innumerable traitors against the public good.  Conspicuous examples are Jefferson and Madison in the eighteenth century, Roger Taney and Robert Lee in the nineteenth, and Lyndon Johnson and Richard Nixon in the twentieth.  Considering the catastrophic expense, stress, blood, alienation, and political division paid by individual Americans for such treacheries, shouldn't it be our common cause to aspire to a better form of government that would replace elective representative democracy?

Project Athena is daunting, but hardly more daunting than was space travel in 1958 when NASA was established.  Rocket science is very, very difficult, but not impossible. Similarly, creating a *deliberation science* that works well in practice may be very, very difficult, but it is hardly impossible. It is not the political equivalent of colonizing the sun. Whether we believe humans were made supernaturally by a mindful God, or that they were made naturally by mindless evolution, we should not judge the search for unknown powers, beauty, and perfections in our humanity to be irrational, anymore than we should judge Euclid, Archimedes, and Euler to be irrational because they went looking for unknown powers, beauty, and perfections in the mathematical world, or Kepler, Newton, and Einstein to be irrational because they went looking for unknown powers, beauty, and perfections in the heavens. Science tells us the human brain is the most sophisticated and complicated thing in all nature, with enormous flexibility and awesome powers well beyond our present, and perhaps even our future, understanding. In contrast, it is often assumed, without experiment or proof, that the people are incapable of moral or political excellence, or devoid of the aspiration to achieve it. But let us spurn the legions of contemporary cynics who would downsize our humanity and, instead, be inspired by eighteenth-century perfectionist aspirations

**Benjamin Rush:** "I am fully persuaded, that from the combined action of causes, which operate at once upon the reason, the moral faculty, the passions, the senses, the brain, the nerves, the blood and the heart, it is possible to produce such a change in the moral character of man, as shall raise him to a resemblance of angels—nay more, to the likeness of God himself."

Whether in the eighteenth-century, or in the twenty-first, patriots of the American Revolution must be patriots of human nature. The leaders of Project Athena will presuppose that there may be unknown civic abilities of humans, and their job is to find them. However, as a point of political integrity, they will never imitate the depraved self-delusion of the Founders, by believing that difficulty, in carrying out a momentous political imperative in the cause of humanity, excuses the enormous dishonor of not trying. Instead, they will imitate the leaders of Project Apollo in treating all difficulties as solvable, if only they would fully exploit the awesome resources of American civilization. Sunshine patriots will no more succeed today than they could have in 1776; Project Athena may have to endure its Valley Forge before the first victory is won.

Since the people in a deliberative frame of mind define the public good, the Agency for Common Reason would begin by creating a number of *advisory juries* whose job it is to answer questions on any political topic that the President or Congress or the Supreme Court might submit to them. Each jury would be randomly chosen from the public, and large enough to insure that the answers will closely match answers the people as a whole would give, were they to deliberate on the questions. Every advisory jury would be put into an environment comparable to a well-run courtroom, where its members would hear opposing arguments whose presentation is governed by fair and impartial rules. That environment, together with the advisory jury members, would be called a *court of common reason*. The design goal would be to construct the best possible ambience for careful reasoning and wise decisions. Each advisory jury would be broken down into *subjuries* of twelve people to deliberate and vote. Every subjury would have its "jury room," which might be actual or virtual (using video-conferencing). The isolation from other subjuries would help protect against the dangers of groupthink that are often found in large gatherings.

**James Madison:** "In all very numerous assemblies, of whatever characters composed, passion never fails to wrest the sceptre from reason. Had every Athenian citizen been a Socrates, every Athenian assembly would still have been a mob."

A decision of a subjury would count only if the decision were unanimous. As in a trial jury, the requirement of unanimity promotes the goal of a considered judgment, since each may have to convince others so that his or her point of view will prevail. The decision of the entire advisory jury would be determined by a plurality of the decisions of those subjuries that achieve unanimity. For instance, suppose an advisory jury of 12,000 people is divided into 1,000 subjuries. On a given question the total of the subjuries might be 487 affirmative, 301 negative, and 212 undecided (unanimity not being achieved in those subjuries). Hence the decision is affirmative. Again, if 10 percent of the subjuries were negative and the rest undecided, the advice would be weakly negative; or if 85 percent of the subjuries were affirmative, the advice would be strongly affirmative. Courts of common reason thus would measure the strength, as well as the quality, of the people's *considered* judgment.

The questions that governmental leaders might pose to advisory juries are almost endless: Is this tax fair and proper? What should legislators earn? Are the poor being treated with dignity? What kinds of information can be kept secret from the public, and for how long? Are congressional districts reasonably drawn? What questions should be put on a census? What should be the punishment for rape? How much of our public resources should go into space exploration? What is the social cost of smoking? Or marijuana? What should be done about CRISPR technology? Or climate change? Should a year of public service be required of high school graduates? How should we respond to this pandemic?

The advisory jury would not decide questions *in vacuo.* For example, before answering questions about medical malpractice, the clash of interests would be made clear: Lawyers representing victims could argue that present procedures are cruel, that they result in inadequate compensation, that doctors are very often sloppy or incompetent, and they could illustrate this in case after case. The members of the medical profession could argue that the number of malpractice suits was preposterous, that forcing doctors and nurses to look at every patient as a legal adversary would result in many unnecessary tests, that the expense of malpractice insurance was pushing medical expenses out of sight, that unrelenting litigation was making the profession unattractive to the next generation. And they could illustrate this in case after case. Consumer groups could also give their arguments. And so on. After that, the advisory jury would decide hypothetical case after hypothetical case of malpractice, in a context where the clashes between insurance costs, on the one hand, and the plight of victims with their traditional rights to sue, on the other hand, were continually highlighted. If jurors set awards too high they would know that their own deductibles and insurance expenses would rise to amounts they deem unaffordable, whether paid directly, or by higher taxes. If they set them too low they would know that victims (perhaps including themselves) would be left with inadequate funds, and little recourse against malpractice. Then, on the basis of the jury's judgments about many hypothetical cases, legislators could devise laws—relying on experts and perhaps aided by artificial intelligence—that best embody the informed values of the public; judges and trial juries could be guided in making awards to victims; insurance companies could more accurately price their insurance; and victims could know when they were getting a fair deal according to the considered judgment of the American people.

Furthermore, decisions would not be determined for all time, but would be periodically revisited, so that a point of view that fails on one occasion may triumph at a later time, when the people's considered judgments have changed. State and local courts would likewise be established. Henceforth, capital letters will be used — *Court of Common Reason* — when a court of common reason statistically represents all the people under a government's jurisdiction (whether federal, state, or local), whereas lower case letters will designate function.

Second-order questions, that is, questions about juries, would also be posed. Juries that answer these questions will be called *metajuries*. For example, a metajury could decide some issue is important enough to justify the time and expense of a deliberative decision by an advisory jury. After an issue has been chosen, a second metajury could approve the questions to be put to the advisory jury. This would protect against manipulation of outcomes using artfully framed questions. Courts of common reason would create an *evidence-based* politics that is self-correcting, as experience teaches what policies are warranted by the evidence, and what are not. Random procedures, metajuries, and the requirement of independent verification, would all be needed to help insure the end result is truly the common reason. The courts represent a new moral and political science and technology that is as subject to misuse as any science and technology is. Hence a major part of Project Athena will be continually devoted to preventing that misuse. It would seek to be highly unlike the Internet, which made the spread of disinformation much easier, and created cybercrime and cyberwar, scourges hitherto unknown.

## SOME USES OF COURTS OF COMMON REASON

**Thomas Jefferson:** From a letter to John Adams: "A general call of ward-meetings . . . on the same day thro' [Virginia] would at any time produce the genuine sense of the people on any required point, and would enable the state to act in mass, as your people have so often done, and with so much effect, by their town meetings."

Although the general idea of *town meetings* is embodied in courts of common reason, the courts differ sharply from the reality of town meetings because in neither eighteenth-century nor contemporary forms are they founded on statistically valid samples of the people. Further, modern town meetings are often directed toward influencing, rather than discovering, the views of the people. They certainly do not provide an appropriate environment for people to deliberate among themselves, much less to demonstrate accurately where the people's considered judgments differ from those of their political leaders. The goal of Project Athena is to "produce the genuine sense of the people on any required point," *not* to create "electronic democracy" in the sense of a continuing electronic poll of the people's non-deliberate opinions. Radio talk shows, interactive television, and the Internet can be as fertile a ground for producing democratic mobs as the village green and, given their size and speed, they are much more dangerous.

Courts of common reason transcend town meetings as much as contemporary laptops transcend the mechanical calculators typically used during World War II. They might become as indispensable for free societies to create moral wealth as computers have been in creating economic wealth. How? First, by posing a number of questions at once. Then political compromises would be possible through vote trading: "I will vote with you on the second question, if you will vote with me on the third." The probability of a subjury being unanimous would thus be increased. This would establish a market whose values are not monetary, but moral and political. It would eliminate the need for moral and political dictators to set public policies, in the way an ordinary competitive market eliminates the need for economic dictators to set prices. It might often allow a plurality to be turned into a majority, and a majority into a consensus, thus forming a more perfect union. A fair and honest economic market among sellers and consumers is one of the most powerful ideas that humans have invented; this concept should guide designing a fair and honest political market among citizens to become a new and revolutionary instrument of conflict resolution.

**James Madison:** "If the United States mean to obtain or deserve the full praise due to wise and just governments, they will equally respect the rights of property, and the property in rights: they will rival the government that most sacredly guards the former; and by repelling its example in violating the latter, will make themselves a pattern to that and all other governments."

To embody American revolutionary aspirations in the twenty-first century, the guiding creed must then become: Free economic exchanges of money, products, and services by sellers and customers in places of business must exist to protect the "rights of property"; but those rights must be checked and balanced by "property in rights" that are determined by markets of free political exchanges of ideas, arguments, and votes by citizens in Courts of Common

Reason. These *Dual Freedoms* Courts, operating with meticulous honesty, can and ought to be the secure foundation of our free economy and our free polity in the twenty-first century. Those Courts makes the terms *capitalism* and *socialism* obsolete by turning the war between them into an ongoing deliberative peace treaty. The privileged of America are right to say that markets are the key to freedom when it comes to "rights of property," but wrong to claim that we need dictators—and most often they are the dictators—when it comes to "property in rights."

**Thomas Jefferson:** "Whenever the people are well-informed, they can be trusted with their own government; . . . whenever things get so far wrong as to attract their notice, they may be relied on to set them to rights."

Here we see an enlargement of the crucial concept of market from economics to include the politics of wards. Hence our Dual Freedoms Courts would continually strive to maintain that equilibrium between "rights of property" and "property in rights" which, in the considered judgment of the people, best promotes public happiness. Over time that would create a level of distributed intelligence unprecedented in human history. To achieve that intelligence would require appropriating the idea of biological evolution into courts of common reason, so they become more like living organisms. Darwin believed he had found the "simple way by which species become exquisitely adapted to various ends."

**Thomas Jefferson:** "The excellence of every government is it's adaptation to the state of those to be governed by it."

**John Adams:** "A perfect constitution of government is so delicate an instrument that I fear no nation will ever have an ear sufficiently exquisite to keep it always in tune."

Since evolution can produce objects of transcendent beauty, subtlety, economy, and functionality, might it not be prudent to learn from Darwin's "simple way" in order to achieve the "adaptation" that Jeffersonian excellence requires? Thus just as it was found that studying dolphins is useful in designing a submarine, or snake fangs in designing a hypodermic needle, perhaps studying brains, self-regulating ecological systems, and synthetic biological creatures would be useful in designing *high-fidelity democracies* that have "sufficiently exquisite" ears always to play in perfect "tune" with the people? By applying biomimicry to the concept of evolution itself, we can create a vigorous, but amicable, competition in Courts of Common Reason in order to prevent the ruthless and violent competition among people that has been so characteristic of human history and prehistory. Project Athena would attempt to engineer a nonviolent equivalent of Darwinian evolution, so that our governments and societies could achieve that transcendent beauty, subtlety, economy, and functionality that we so often find in nature.

Consider a simplified thought experiment to explain the concept of a *democratic evolutionary design*. Suppose federal public policy on drugs must be decided. Now imagine that eight individuals or organizations each submit a different proposed policy on drugs to a Court of Common Reason. After discussing all the proposals, the jurors vote and reject one of them in the first round (the political equivalent of *natural selection*). In the second round, the sponsors of the remaining seven proposals examine what has been accepted and rejected, and then they may modify their proposals, if they wish, for resubmission to the Court (the political equivalent of *descent with modification*). The Court then eliminates one more proposal, reducing the remaining ones to six. The process continues for five more rounds when there will be just one surviving proposal, the political outcome of successive designs generated through intelligent variation by proposers, and successive choices generated through mindful deliberation by the people. (Biological outcomes, in sharp contrast, are produced by successive designs generated through random variation and mindless natural selection.) The surviving proposal would become the public policy on drugs.

A women falls asleep on her arm and it becomes completely numb. She wakes up and asks: "Is this *my* arm?" She has briefly lost the *proprioceptive sense* that her arm is hers. The deliberate sense of the people would be, as it were, the proprioceptive sense in the body politic because Courts of Common Reason would maintain an exact, ergonomic relation between the people and their own government. The numbness of political alienation—"Is this my country?"—would be reduced, even disappear when the government achieves robust political competence. Whenever the *primary* authority of the people has use of an institution that embodies the democratic evolutionary design, there is no need for special creation of public policy by *secondary* authority, such as legislators, judges, governors, or presidents. If Project Athena were successful, our governments would reach degrees of excellence in adaptation and tuning that Jefferson and Adams could not have envisaged.

That excellence would enable an utterly new means of conflict resolution. For instance, suppose a large jury is formed consisting of people of one race. Operating as usual, the jury answers a set of political questions. Independently, and in the same time frame, a second advisory jury of equal size is formed consisting of people of a different race. The members answer the same questions. A set of issues on which the deliberate sense of the two races actually differ is thereby identified. Then the two advisory juries are merged into one hybrid jury, where each subjury consists of twelve people, six from each group. The issues on which the two races differ are then presented at the same time, and compromises are made via vote trading within each subjury. The decisions of the hybrid jury, if approved by a Court of Common Reason and Congress, would resolve the political issues for a given time in the same sense in which an ordinary election resolves who will serve for a given time. After all the millennia of conflict among races or sexes or social classes or countries, would it not be wise to collect solid evidence as to where, *after due deliberation and reflection*, the groups in each of these categories actually differ from one another (since our expectations here might be wildly wrong), and then let the members of the subgroups themselves, rather than their leaders, make any necessary compromises? Whether for our riven country or riven world, hybrid juries might often be the only reliable and peaceful mechanism for conflict resolution. Wouldn't it have been wonderful if, from the beginning, there had been local, state, national and international Courts of Common Reason to deal with the COVID-19 pandemic instead of the oligarchic dishonesty and oligarchic incompetency that humanity generally received? Perhaps the initial epidemic might never have become a pandemic.

## THE COLLECTIVE INTELLIGENCE OF ADVISORY JURIES

It might be thought that ordinary people are not intelligent enough to serve successfully on courts of common reason, much less capable of creating an unprecedented level of distributed intelligence. This objection does not seem reasonable for certain kinds of questions—Should *America, the Beautiful* replace the *Star Spangled Banner* as our national anthem?—but it does seem plausible for many other kinds. We can begin to answer this objection with an intuitive explanation of the Condorcet Jury Theorem (1785) in mathematics. This Theorem, along with its generalizations, and related development, forms the statistical basis of democracy. Suppose elementary students are given a yes-no numerical question, such as "Is 31 a prime number?" They work independently, put their "yes " or "no" answers on a piece of paper, and then, one by one, "cast their ballots" in a box. For each student, suppose the chance of giving the right answer is 80%. Then as the number of "votes" in the box increase, we could say with greater and greater confidence that the percent of right answers to the total number of "ballots" in the box will increasingly get closer to 80%. This means that we could say with greater and greater confidence that the majority of "votes" in the box is correct.

The Condorcet Jury Theorem is a mathematically exact version of this kind of reasoning. According to it, if, as above, the probability that each voter is right is 80% then, if there are at least thirteen voters, the probability that the majority is right is greater than 99%. Let us make an extremely conservative assumption about the civic capabilities of Americans. Suppose each unanimous subjury has a mere 51% chance of being right, barely better than chance. Call any subjury *qualified* if it meets that low standard. The theorem tells us that in an advisory jury of 13,627 qualified subjuries, with a majority of 6814 unanimous subjuries (1/2 x 13,627 = 6813.5), the jury will be right 99% of the time, but just barely. Notice that barely 99% is a good start, but is not enough. If we only achieved a 99% standard of airplane flights without a crash, we would have hundreds of crashes each day. The Federal Aviation Administration made aviation much safer, not by stopping accidents, but by stopping repeated accidents for the same cause. The Agency for Common Reason would do the same for political decisions. If a Court of Common Reason makes a mistake, as judged by a subsequent Court, it would be investigated with the kind of diligence used in airplane mishaps, in order to ultimately make bad political decisions at least as rare as those mishaps.

Project Athena would devise experiments to learn how to increase the collective intelligence of advisory juries in practice. Deliberative competence in politics can be understood by studying deliberations in areas where a correct answer is well-defined, such as crossword puzzles, detective stories, predictions of future events, mathematics, logic, medicine, engineering, and the like. The experience of devising successful systems for a variety of topics in which correct answers are known would then be used in devising systems for political questions, where answers are often controversial. By *successful* I mean cases in which the knowledge and talents of each individual in a subjury may be unlikely to get the correct answer, but where the probability that unanimous judgment, after deliberation, is right would be 51% or higher. The greater the divergence between individual and collective achievement, the greater the success of the deliberative system. Consider an intelligence test where each member of the jury has an IQ of 100; what would be the maximum *collective* intelligence that could be achieved in practice? The fact that political decisions often involve judgments of preference or value does not mean that these judgments are not subject to deliberative reason. For example, an initial preference to lynch a person without a fair trial could be examined by considering whether the following factual proposition is true: *If the person is lynched without a fair trial, then public happiness will be harmed in the longer term.* If the common reason of society judges that proposition to be true, then the starting preference ought not to be fulfilled, *even if the preference remains.*

**James Madison:** The decisions of society should be "controuled by subjecting the will of the society to the reason of society."

Courts of Common Reason are designed to frustrate the "will of society" whenever it is contrary to the "reason of society." They give many opportunities to measure and increase the quality of collective decisions. How? Well, we might test whether a new computer program is mathematically sound by using it to calculate the decimal expansion of $\pi$, because the those decimals are already known to a precision of billions of digits. Similarly, exercises in critical thinking, where answers are known, could verify that advisory juries have the collective intelligence that is necessary to deliberate on political questions. For instance, imagine an advisory jury where each subjury practices on exercises in critical thinking until it reaches an x level of deliberating competence on questions with well-defined answers. Next, the subjuries answer a series of questions concerning political issues. After that, each of the subjuries among the winning juries again achieves level x of deliberating competence We could then assert that the answers given for the political issues had been authenticated by a *sandwich* of deliberative competence at level x.

In practice there will be many complications compared to my idealized examples. How could a large number of proposals be handled in a real case where there are constraints of time and money?

What are the optimal number of alternatives to offer subjurors, so they do not become hindered by too few choices, or overwhelmed by too many? There may be jurors who are unfruitful (right, but incapable of convincing anyone else), or dogmatic (no discussion will change their minds), or amenable (always trying to vote with the majority), or rebellious (always creating a minority or voting with one), or apathetic (whose votes approximate randomness), or true deliberators (whose final judgment is determined by their own deliberate discernment). Traditionally, deliberation was a requirement meant to kill off unfavorable ideas, as were the additional requirements of being cool and unanimous. As far as practical, Project Athena would be structured to promote every epistemological virtue, while frustrating every epistemological vice, so that the "will of society" would never be contrary to the "reason of society."

In nature the evolutionary principle is mindless and brutal; in courts of common reason it is mindful and caring; *ideas* are subjected to a repeated, evolutionary competition so only the fittest survives, fittest, that is, at promoting the flourishing of a free and independent people. Hence the people need constantly to improve their deliberative skill, so that they can create the conditions for political excellence that alone will reliably protect the human animal against itself.

## ATHENA

The advisory jury system is a generalization of the ordinary trial jury system, in that facts about considered judgments of the people in general are discovered, instead of just facts applying to a particular case, such as whether or not a specific defendant is guilty.

Unlike many proposals for participatory democracy, Project Athena would relentlessly give efficiency a high priority. For instance, a set of courts could operate simultaneously on different aspects of the same question. Just as creating superfast computers requires parallel processing, where a number of computations are carried out simultaneously by different microprocessors, so the efficient determination of the common reason of society requires *parallel deliberation*, where different groups of subjuries deliberate on different aspects of the question at the same time.

Americans would draft themselves into jury duty.by having metajuries determine the schedule, pace, and duration of that duty. These are the limits within which Project Athena must work. Who says we cannot be as clever at saving human energy in making deliberative decisions, as we have been in saving physical energy by using robots, or nature has been in saving mental energy in the brain? Hence, after courts of common reason generate large amounts of data—"big data"—it should be possible, using computer simulation, to create an accurate dynamic model of the moral and political character of the American people. Let us call this model *Athena*, and give her a voice, à la Siri or Alexa, that could guide the President, members of Congress, and Supreme Court justices as they do their job. They could ask Athena for suggestions about how to improve the laws and operation of the government, a sophisticated version of the way computers suggest books to read based on the information they have about you. They might also ask Athena, of each prospective law, what unintended and undesirable consequences it might have, were the law passed. Athena would be a deep learner with excellent explanatory powers to articulate in human terms the reasons for her suggestions.

**James Wilson:** "In free states, the people form an artificial person or body politick, the highest and noblest that can be known. They form that moral person, which [is] . . . a complete body of free natural persons, united together for their common benefit; as having an understanding and a will; as deliberating, and resolving, and acting; as possessed of interests which it ought to manage; as enjoying rights which it ought to maintain; and as lying under obligations which it ought to perform. To this moral person, we assign, by way of eminence, the dignified appellation of *state*."

Athena is meant to be a twenty-first-century embodiment of Wilson's "moral person," that is, a virtual person that reflects the common reason of the American people. As patriots of 1776 we are patriots of human nature, we must look there for unknown powers, beauty, and perfection. Isn't it ironic that, while boasting that America is the greatest democracy in human history, we spend untold billions to engineer the maximum possible artificial intelligence, but spend little to engineer the maximum possible civic intelligence in the American people? Project Athena may not succeed, but the philosophy of the American Revolution requires that we keep trying even with multiple early failures.

The aim would be to engineer a democracy that combines actual analog democracy, using human deliberation, with virtual digital democracy, using computer simulations. We could say: "As the virtual people calculate and the actual people deliberate, so the political world will be." This is a paraphrase of Leibniz: "As God calculates and thinks, so the universe will be." I paraphrase Leibniz to make clear that a democracy based on Courts of Common Reason is a contemporary embodiment of the revolutionary American idea that the common reason of the people rightfully has God-like authority in establishing and maintaining the state.

In this eighteenth-century conception "God-like authority" does not include actions that are morally wrong.  For example, in the Bible God makes an agreement with Noah that is universal: "I establish my covenant with you; that never again shall all flesh be cut off by the waters of a flood, and never again shall there be a flood to destroy the earth."  God became a ruler bound by his own agreements; even he cannot commit worldwide genocide again.  In fact, when he wished to destroy just Sodom and Gomorrah, Abraham objected: "Shall not the Judge of all the earth do right?"  Or consider what the Lord said to Moses, "I have seen this people, and behold, it is a stiff-necked people; now therefore let me alone, that my wrath may burn hot against them and I may consume them."  But Moses objects that God cannot do so without violating his own promises. He begs God to "turn from thy fierce wrath, and repent of this evil against thy people. . . . And the Lord repented of the evil which he thought to do to his people."  Although God had the power to violate his moral law, he didn't have the right.  Neither does the *demos*.

**Thomas Jefferson**: The "people in mass . . . are inherently independent of all but moral law."

Of course, by the "people in mass" Jefferson did not mean a democratic mob on the village green, but the "common reason of the society" as revealed in ward meetings.  To fulfill this conception today, it must be up to the people to decide periodically, via metajuries, what first-order decisions should be virtual and what actual, and then how often virtual decisions by Athena should be checked for their fidelity to actual first-order judgments by the American people.  Let us now suppose that Project Athena achieves its mission of constructing Athena to be an excellent, virtual advisor to Congress, an advice that precisely reflects the considered views of the American people. Even this stupendous achievement would not be enough to satisfy a legislative standard of the American Revolution. That standard was Athenian (as described by Aristotle): "The appointment of magistrates by lot is thought to be democratic, and the election of them oligarchical." A "characteristic of democracy [is] . . . to rule and be ruled in turns; and so it contributes to the freedom based upon equality." "For if liberty and equality, as is thought by some, are chiefly to be found in democracy, they will be best attained when all persons alike share in the government to the utmost." The Americans described both their Athenian dreams and their inability to live up to them.

**James Wilson:** "The Gov$^t$ ought to possess not only 1st. the *force* but 2ndly. the *mind* or sense of the people at large. The Legislature ought to be the most exact transcript of the whole Society. Representation is made necessary only because it is impossible for the people to act collectively."

**John Adams (April 1776):** A "Representative Assembly . . . should be in miniature, an exact portrait of the people at large. It should think, feel, reason, and act like them." This Assembly will occur "naturally, when all the powers of government come to be in the hands of the people's friends."

**Thomas Jefferson:** A *republic* means "a government by its citizens in mass, acting directly and personally, according to rules established by the majority; and that every other government is more or less republican, in proportion as it has in its composition more or less of this ingredient of the direct action of its citizens. Such a government is evidently restrained to very narrow limits of space and population. I doubt it would be practicable beyond the extent of a

New England township."

We must distinguish between the *elective representative* Congress that was actually achieved in 1787, and the *statistical representative* legislature that perfect democratic republics should have. Let our thought experiment to revive the American Revolution create a *Court of Common Reason Congress* (henceforth *CCR Congress*) in which *oligarchic* elective representation is replaced by a *democratic* statistical representation whose members would "rule and be ruled in turns" in order to perfectly embody "liberty and equality." The resulting laws would have great authority both because they express "the *mind* or sense of the people" *and* they would be made in the careful and responsible way required by all Courts of Common Reason. Efficiency would dictate parallel deliberation using many CCR Congresses, where each is limited to a specific topic set by a national metajury, and each would aim at the precision, simplicity, beauty, and perspicuity that all laws should have.

In addition, our courts "should think, feel, reason, and act like" the American people. To achieve that, an ordinary jury would decide, and a metajury would rule on whether an appeal could be made. After that, the initial decision could only be overruled by a larger jury, and so on up to the *CCR Supreme Court,* which would be a Court of Common Reason. The desperate need for a CCR court system is easily seen.

**John Adams:** "I never knew a Jury, by a Verdict, to determine a Negro to be a Slave. They always found them free."

In sharp contrast, our oligarchic Supreme Court always found them slaves until the Civil War, and then subject to peonage or Jim Crow until the 1960s. Isn't this colossal failure to judge in the cause of humanity over such a long period of time enough to prove that something is radically wrong with our appellate court system? No rational person would accept the rule of law where that law could authorize hereditary slavery, or hereditary peonage—rightly called "slavery by another name" by Douglas Bowman—or hereditary Jim Crow, or any other moral abomination, such as Herod's decree. A rational person could certainly embrace a democratic republic, where unjust laws could always be obstructed by randomly chosen juries.

**Thomas Jefferson:** The "republican is the only form of government which is not eternally at open or secret war with the rights of mankind." In the draft of the Declaration Jefferson accused George III of waging "cruel war against human nature itself" by making slaves of Africans. Elsewhere he found southerners "aristocratical, . . . zealous for their own liberties, but trampling on those of others."

**James Madison:** "The transcendent law of nature and of nature's God, which declares that the safety and happiness of society, are the objects at which all political institutions aim, and to which all such institutions must be sacrificed." "In proportion as slavery prevails in a State, the Government, however democratic in name, must be aristocratic in fact. . . . All the antient popular governments, were for this reason aristocracies. The majority were slaves. . . . The Southern States of America, are on the same principle aristocracies."

**Luther Martin:** "*Slavery* is *inconsistent* with the *genius* of *republicanism.*"

**David Barrow:** "The Author, from . . . a discovery of the inconsistancy of hereditary slavery, with a republican form of government, manumitted his slaves in the year 1784."

**The Constitution (1787):** The "United States shall

guarantee to every state in this union a Republican form of government."

No state can be republican if there could be a revolution against it, rightly justified by the Declaration of Independence. That justification will always be furnished by a state that supports hereditary slavery. Further, if there can be no hereditary slaves, there can be no hereditary masters, nobles, or kings. Such hereditary advantages and disadvantages are ruled out by the Declaration and the Constitution. Yet neither the courts, nor the Congresses, nor the Presidents of the founding generation were willing to obey the Declaration's "Laws of Nature and of Nature's God" or the Constitution's republican guarantee—both of which they swore to uphold—in order to sacrifice on the altar of freedom the aristocratic laws supporting slavery and other practices contrary to natural right.

Today the Supreme Court exhibits a similar willingness to preside over an oligarchic republic rather than a democratic one. For instance, in 2000 Susette Kelo's home was threatened by eminent domain for subsequent private use by a corporation. She found that Connecticut law, in its majestic legal equality, graciously allowed the poor as well as the rich to keep their property by successfully suing the state. No other defense was allowed, certainly no trial by jury.

**Delaware legislature (1766):** "Trial by Jury [is] the great Preservative of public Liberty and private Property."

**The Declaration of Independence:** The "King of Great Britain" is accused of "depriving us in many cases, of the benefits of Trial by Jury."

With substantial help, Kelo *was* able to sue. When the case reached the Supreme Court, the decision gave New London "broad latitude in determining what public needs justify the use of the takings power"; thus that power over poor, but not rich, homeowners was absolute; the poor had no ownership rights that New London had to respect, because their "property in rights" were ignored.

**The United States Constitution:** "The right of the people to be secure in their persons, houses, papers, and effects, against unreasonable searches and seizures, shall not be violated."

**Gouverneur Morris:** "The Constitution of the United States has reserved to every citizen the inalienable right of a trial by his peers in every case affecting his life, his liberty, or his property."

**The oath of Supreme Court judges:** "I will administer justice without respect to persons, and do equal right to the poor and to the rich."

Abuses of eminent domain—Kelo was not "secure" in her home—would be eliminated by using Dual Freedoms Courts of Common Reason to set the standards for "searches and seizures" of "persons, houses, papers, and effects"; then having a local jury determine that the standards had been met in specific cases. Without juries, there is no security of property, no equal protection of the laws, no economic justice, no democratic republic.

It gets worse. John Thompson spent eighteen years in the Louisiana State Penitentiary, fourteen of them on death row. He was released when it was discovered that evidence that prosecutors had suppressed, exonerated him. In 2011 he sued. A jury awarded him $14 million, one million for every year on death row. Here members of a jury representing the people of Louisiana said that they were willing to pay a very substantial sum out of their own pocket (via taxes or fines) for the enormous injustice of their government's fraudulently taking eighteen years of Thompson's freedom. (As it later turned out, this equaled one-third of his lifetime.) In an act of stunning antidemocratic usurpation, the Supreme Court ruled that the people did not have the right to spend their own money to compensate Thompson for this despicable crime by prosecutors. Rather the Court decided that justice required that Thompson get nothing and the prosecutors not be punished. As it so often did, oligarchy triumphed in the Supreme Court.

**James Madison:** "The cool and deliberate sense of the community ought in all governments, and actually will in all free governments ultimately prevail over the views of its rulers."

The Supreme Court violates democratic republican standards because five justices in a divided nine-person Supreme Court can "ultimately prevail" over the "cool and deliberate sense" of a unanimous twelve-person trial jury. The Court also presides over a judicial branch where only a few percent get jury trials.

**The United States Constitution:** "The Trial of all Crimes, except in Cases of Impeachment, shall be by Jury."

The states likewise can be contemptuous of juries. In Alabama, for example, judges have changed a jury's decision for life imprisonment to execution over a hundred times since 1976. Would it not be a test of our honest commitment to a free society, of our powers of political innovation, of our technological imagination, of our organizational prowess, and of our perfectionist aspirations in the cause of humanity, to see if Project Athena could design a judicial branch, with both virtual and real trials, that would truly fulfill the spirit and words of our Declaration and Constitution? In 2017 the computer program AlphaZero was given the rules of chess, and then played against itself millions of times to become unbeatable within hours. The Agency for Common Reason would try to devise experiments to see if the rules of justice could be derived from the common reason of the people, and then, *mutatis mutandis,* have computers play against themselves until they could play the game of justice with such (software) engineering excellence that virtual trials of actual disputes become cheap, useful, and ubiquitous.

Indeed the practicality of this kind of engineering would extend far beyond the state. Thus a large company might use it to find the greatest simultaneous satisfaction for employees, customers, and shareholders. *Mutatis mutandis*, the same could be said of churches, foundations, unions, professional organizations, and so forth. Eventually courts of common reason might have advantages that at present we cannot conceive, much less exploit. None of the early pioneers in computers thought they would be used for word processing, for on-board navigation of rockets, or the Internet. Again, we should be clear, the problems of creating American governments that continually improve their achievable degree of perfection are so vast that deliberation science will, so to say, be rocket science; that is, arduous but doable.

The resources available for Project Athena to achieve eighteenth-century dreams are enormous. Large numbers of colleges and universities might set up *Departments of Deliberation Science*, in part paid for by numerous public-spirited foundations. Further expertise could be found in such organizations as IBM, Microsoft, Apple, Google, Amazon, Facebook, A. C. Nielsen, the American Institute of Public Opinion (Gallup), the Educational Testing Service, the American Bar Association, the Library of Congress, the Census Bureau, The Museum of the American Revolution, debating societies, and so forth. Relying on such talent, the Agency for Common Reason could experiment, by instituting protocols to promote serious discussions, increase collective intelligence, prevent manipulation of outcomes, reduce emotions contrary to reason, increase passions for truth and justice, provide for independent confirmation of results, and devise self-corrective mechanisms when mistakes are made. A people that supports the aspiration for democratic perfection, and regularly corrects their own mistakes, is truly self-governing, worthy of the exalted names *sovereign, free, equal, independent, autonomous.*

For more than half a century, we have spent vast sums on the effort to produce a controlled and useful thermonuclear reaction. Why did we not commit equal time and funds to explore the common reason of the American people? The answer is the widespread belief that such reason, if it could be said to exist at all, is a worthless "lowest common denominator." We believe in things mechanical and quantum mechanical, but not in humans free and rational. This is, as it were, racism against the human race—a ubiquitous "soft bigotry of low expectations"(G.W. Bush)—the radical opposite of the philosophy of the American Revolution.

**John Adams:** The founding generation relied on the "integrity and intelligence of the people, under an overruling Providence."

**Thomas Jefferson:** "The cherishment of the people . . . was our principle."

Aristotle said that "there is something beyond the bodies that are about us on this earth, different and separate from them; and that the superior glory of its nature is proportionate to its distance from this world of ours." This dichotomy between the "superior glory" of the heavens and "this world of ours" was also common in Christianity. For example, it was adopted by Copernicus. His book, *On the Revolutions of Heavenly Spheres* (1543), begins: "Among the many various literary and artistic pursuits which invigorate men's minds, the strongest affection and utmost zeal should, I think, promote the studies concerned with the most beautiful objects, most deserving to be known." Since those "most beautiful objects, most deserving to be known" were the "heavenly spheres" created by God, astronomy was a "divine rather than human science." The Americans made no such distinction:

**John Adams:** "There can be no employment more agreeable to a benevolent mind, than a research after the best" in "the divine science of politicks."

**James Wilson:** "Man . . . may be preserved, improved, and perfected. The celestial as well as the terrestrial world knows its exalted but prescribed course."

These views were influenced by certain parts of the Bible: "In the beginning God created the heavens and the earth." "God created man in his own image." "I *am* the Almighty God; walk before me, and be thou perfect." "Ye shall be holy: for I the Lord your God *am* holy." "Be ye therefore perfect, even as your Father which is in heaven is perfect."

Hence the soaring aesthetic spirit that made the heliocentrism of Copernicus so intensively attractive and perfectionist applies not just to the heavens, but to the earth and its humans. In 1656, James Harrington, one of John Adams favorite authors, made this scientific optimism explicitly political: "And if reason be nothing else but interest, and the interest of mankind be the right interest, then the reason of mankind must be right reason. Now compute well, for if the interest of popular government come the nearest unto the interest of mankind, then the reason of popular government must come nearest unto right reason." "As the form of a man is the image of

God, so the form of a government is the image of man." For Harrington, then, the Creator of Nature is Nature's God, whereas the Creator of Popular Government (that is, the people), is Government's God.

**The Declaration of Independence:** "When in the Course of human Events, it becomes necessary for One People to dissolve the Political Bands which have connected them with another, and to assume among the Powers of the Earth, the separate and equal Station to which the Laws of Nature and of Nature's God entitle them, a decent Respect to the Opinions of Mankind requires that they should declare the causes which impel them to the Separation."

The Americans believed that perfections found in the heavens by mathematical astronomy could be matched by perfections found in the people by deliberative politics. This explains why, if a "Representative Assembly" is "an exact portrait of the people at large"(Adams) or a "Legislature" is "the most exact transcript of the whole Society"(Wilson), then the "deliberate sense of the community"(Madison) or "the common reason of the society"(Jefferson) that is expressed by such governments becomes a revelation of the sublime rational beauty associated with God and Nature. Here are two passages from eighteenth-century sermons.

**Jonathan Mayhew:** "It is principally on account of our reason, that we are said to have been *created in the image of God.*" (Note the Bible: "Come now, let us reason together, says the Lord.")

**Nathanael Emmons:** "The dignity of man appears from his bearing the *image* of his Maker. . . . His soul is a transcript of the *natural* perfections of the Deity. God is a spirit, and so is the soul of man; God is intelligence and activity, and so is the soul of man. In a word, man is the living image of the living God . . . The truth is, rationality is the same in all intelligent beings. Reason is the same thing in God, in Angels, and in Men. As men therefore bear the *image* of God, in point of Rationality; so they possess all the *rational* powers and faculties, which bear any analogy to the divine intelligence." (No racism against the human race here, nor any in the Declaration, as Lincoln explained. The representatives of the people "in old Independence Hall" gave a "majestic interpretation of the economy of the Universe. This was their lofty, and wise, and noble understanding of the justice of the Creator to His creatures. Yes, gentlemen, to *all* His creatures, to the whole great family of man. In their enlightened belief, nothing stamped with the Divine image and likeness was sent into the world to be troden on, and degraded, and imbruted by its fellows. They grasped not only the whole race of man then living, but they reached forward and seized upon the farthest posterity.")

As it was understood when created, American government was to be an ongoing experiment of political engineering, driven by both scientific and Judeo-Christian perfectionism. Newtonian science reveals that the mathematical beauty of heavenly gravity is identical to that of earthly gravity (contradicting Aristotle); whereas "the divine science of politicks" reveals that the moral beauty of God is the same as the moral beauty of humans, who are made in his image. Each and every human being is an imperfect reflection of God, but imperfect in different ways. Imagine some complicated object that could not be viewed directly, but only through a set of irregular mirrors each of which distorted the object's appearance in a different way. By knowing the laws of reflection and refraction, and by carefully studying the various distorted images one could produce a knowledge of the object that was much less distorted than any of its many images. Each mirror would be important in that rational reconstruction. From this point of view, the physical sciences reveal the perfectionist character of God's intellect in nature, while virtuous republics reveal the perfectionist character of God's will in the people. Nature's God and Humanity's God are identical and thus the "celestial as well as the terrestrial world knows its exalted but prescribed course."

**Declaration of Independence:** "We hold these Truths to be self-evident, that all Men are created equal, that they are endowed by their Creator with certain unalienable Rights, that among these are Life, Liberty, and the Pursuit of Happiness." (Note the Bible: "Ye shall know the truth and the truth shall make you free.")

"Happiness" here does not mean a sense of pleasure and satisfaction that even malevolent people might typically feel during a long and successful life of crime. Rather it is based on Aristotle's conception that "happiness is activity in accordance with excellence" and thus politicians should aim at making citizens "good and capable of noble acts." However, the American conception elevated this terrestrial activity to match heavenly glory, and presupposes all humans as capable of it. To be happy means using practical wisdom in the strenuous pursuit of moral excellence to the utmost extent possible, given one's talents and situation. In Cicero's words: "The mere search for higher happiness, not merely its actual attainment, is a prize beyond all human wealth or honour or physical pleasure." Let us listen and learn from the greatest American revolutionist:

**George Washington:** On July 2, 1776, Washington sent general orders to his army: "Let us therefore rely upon the goodness of the Cause, and the aid of the supreme Being, in whose hands Victory is, to animate and encourage us to great and noble Actions."

(Washington had *Cato*, a tragedy of virtue and honor, performed for his troops at Valley Forge.) Elsewhere he says: "There is no truth more thoroughly established, than that there exists in the œconomy and course of nature, an indissoluble union between virtue and happiness, between duty and advantage, between the genuine maxims of an honest and magnanimous policy, and the solid rewards of public prosperity and felicity." "It will be worthy of a free, enlightened, and, at no distant period, a great Nation, to give mankind the magnanimous and too novel example of a people always guided by an exalted justice and benevolence."

*American happiness* is a pursuit that is founded on virtue ethics; and it can be justified today even for those skeptical of all religious claims, which they may view as jam-packed with epistemological vices and moral abominations. Thus we know from secular biology that humans are the product of billions of years of evolution, and are the most resourceful animals in nature, with a surprising consciousness that gives them individual and social identities we have yet to comprehend. It hardly makes sense to assume, *without meticulous empirical investigation*, that ordinary people, who possess these magnificent brains, must, regardless of their experience and education, be incompetent to carry out the jury duties of citizens in a democratic republic. Project Athena, like Project Apollo, gives believers and skeptics a chance to unite, for neither project requires religious assumptions, but Project Athena is likely to uncover truths about God and humans (for the believers), or just about humans (for the skeptics), that could not be discovered in any other way. Should we not here be intensely curious?

On the analogy of a juried art show, let us define a *juried democracy* to be a government where the laws have the continuing, informed consent of the people acting through juries in Courts of Common Reason. In the 1940s and 50s, analog machines—for all their virtues—were completely inadequate for the large-scale calculations that science, business, and the military then needed; a digital electronics was the only way to achieve the required calculating accuracy, reliability, and economy. Similarly, elective representative democracy—for all its virtues—is absolutely incapable of the large-scale deliberations that political science, economics, and down-to-earth politics now need; a juried democracy is the only way to go. Moving from the rule of persons to the rule of law was a radical improvement in the organization of societies; moving on to the rule of juried law will be a no less revolutionary enhancement.

As safety and economy in contemporary travel requires replacing compasses based on magnetism with global positioning systems (GPS) based on satellites, so the pursuit of public happiness in contemporary politics requires replacing *moral compasses* based on tradition with *ethical positioning systems* (EPS) based on Athena. Today, with GPS technology, we can know, with much greater accuracy than was hitherto possible, where we are on the earth; tomorrow, with EPS technology, we will be able to know, with much greater accuracy than is now possible, where we are ethically. The road to political happiness cannot be known without twenty-first-century precision in creating a cognitive map of the moral and political landscape formed by the common reason of the people.

**John Adams:** "The systems of legislators are experiments made on human life and manners, society and government. Zoroaster, Confucius, Mithras, Odin, Thor, Mahomet, Lycurgus, Solon, Romulus, and a thousand others, may be compared to philosophers making experiments on the elements. Unhappily, political experiments cannot be made in a laboratory, nor determined in a few hours."

Adams is here describing an eighteenth-century conception of legislation as a science, where legislative efforts are seen as experiments, and wise legislators base their experiments on careful observation of all human history so as not to repeat past mistakes. By adding computer modeling to history, Project Athena can do what Adams could not have imagined, namely, to conduct "political experiments . . . in a laboratory," whose outcome could perhaps sometimes be "determined in a few hours." More accurate measurements have again and again made possible great advances and mighty revolutions in science and technology; the same holds true for political science and politics.

But we haven't learned this simple lesson. We use a kind of plurality voting in which it is possible for a very liberal candidate to get 24% of the vote, and the remaining four very conservative candidates each get 19%. The liberal wins even though opposed by 76% of the voters. This flaw has been understood for centuries; yet our legislators continue to allow outcomes caused by this artifact of a bad voting system. It results in governmental disinformation when the winner is treated as the genuine democratic choice. Plurality voting further corrupts the electoral process by encouraging people, who actually favor an unpopular candidate, to misrepresent their choice in order not to "throw away their vote." Again, a five-star system for restaurants gives the customers the power to *grade* them (4.3, say), rather than only *rank* them (restaurant x is better than restaurant y). Plurality voting gives only the weaker power of ranking. Yet grading candidates is important. Isn't it obvious that democracy is in better shape where, in elections, it is typical for the winner and the runner-up to be in the fours (say, 4.8 beats a 4.5), than one where the winner is in the twos (say, 2.7 beats 2.3)?

Further, when a presidential election is very close.our voting system is vulnerable to having the popular winner lose. This great risk is wholly self-inflicted. Imagine that the country is divided into 10,000 winner-take-all voting districts of equal population. Then let the victor in the largest number of districts be elected, and the fact there are so many districts would virtually both eliminate ambiguity in close elections and guarantee the popular winner wins. Finally, our party primaries are often protracted in time, arbitrary in design, undemocratic in outcome, and the elections themselves are subject to carelessness in counting, malfunctioning or hackable voting machines, long voting lines, and capricious decisions concerning when ballots, either in person or by mail, are admissible. All this toying demonstrates cynical disrespect for the people. Beautiful design is not needed; slop, slop, slop is good enough for government work; the aspiration for the progressive Newtonian accuracy of the founding generation is unknown; and then there is plenty of self-deluded chutzpah to call this masquerade *democracy*. The pages of Plato no longer contain the greatest satire of democracy, now it is reenacted every four years in our presidential elections.

*Flawless transmission of information* on the moral and political landscape used in EPS technology would transform our unsavory and slipshod politics into the sublime science and beautiful engineering that the Founders envisioned and sometimes practiced. Were our eighteenth-century ancestors able to see our scientific and technological prowess, they would surely be dazzled speechless, but they would hardly be impressed by our Congress as compared to theirs. "Why," they might ask us, "if you are willing to spend untold billions to create self-driving cars, are you not willing to spend even more to create a truly self-legislating people?" Were they among us today, they would likely try to create a CCR Congress; for then their majestic dreams of a perfect self-government would be practiced with an excellence they could conceive, but had few means to achieve.

**James Madison:** "The destined career of my country will exhibit a Government pursuing the public good as its sole object, . . . a Government . . . whose conduct within and without may bespeak the most noble of all ambitions — that of promoting peace on earth and good will to man."

If we keep our contemporary cynicism about the possibility of democratic excellence, we will interpret Madison's conviction to be a union of patriotic puffery and utopian delusion. But if we seek to construct *his* vision of a government meticulously engineered to follow the deliberate sense of the people, *his* "destined career" becomes *our* greatly challenging, but approachable goal. Even with transcendently more financial and human resources than the eighteenth century possessed, must our digital age be so lacking in imagination or so small-souled in spirit, as not to even think, much less seriously try, to make the United States into a juried government that, in practice, would continually pursue "the public good as its sole object," and constantly strive for "peace on earth and good will to man"?

## THE LIBERAL ARTS AND SCIENCES

**Benjamin Rush:** "The form of government we have assumed, has created a new class of duties to every American. It becomes us, therefore, . . . to adapt our modes of teaching to the peculiar form of our government."

So what kind of education do the people need to prepare them to make fateful decisions in a juried democracy? The answer is the *liberal arts and sciences*, which by definition implant whatever knowledge, habits, passions, manners, and ideals are needed or desirable for a free person in a free society to have a flourishing life. The idea of a juried democracy was unknown in the Italian Renaissance, but the kind of education needed for it to prosper was beautifully articulated by Petrus Paulus Vergerius (1370-1444): "We call those studies *liberal* which are worthy of a free man; those studies by which we attain and practise virtue and wisdom; that education which calls forth, trains and develops these highest gifts of body and of mind which ennoble men, and which are rightly judged to rank next in dignity to virtue only." Although Vergerius was unheard of in eighteenth-century America, his general view of a proper education for a free person was certainly expressed.

**James Wilson:** "Where liberty prevails, the arts and sciences lift up their heads and flourish. Where the arts and sciences flourish, political and moral improvements will likewise be made. All will receive from each, and each will receive from all, mutual support and assistance: mutually supported and assisted, all may be carried to a degree of perfection hitherto unknown; perhaps hitherto not believed."

Typically today students are considered liberally educated if, over twelve years of secondary education and four years of college, they receive some training in a large variety of disciplines, such as civics and physical education, logic and mathematics, physics and chemistry, astronomy and biology, anthropology and economics, history and philosophy, literature and religion, the arts and languages, law and engineering. A liberal education should expose students to this kind of variety, together with the know-how to pursue any other discipline whenever they wished. Since a juried democracy creates "a new class of duties to every American" we must "adapt our modes of teaching" to emphasize civic duty, and perhaps "all may be carried to a degree of perfection hitherto unknown; perhaps hitherto not believed."

**John Adams:** "Laws for the liberal education of youth, especially of the lower class of people, are so extremely wise and useful, that, to a humane and generous mind, no expense for this purpose would be thought extravagant." Adams writes to a friend in New Jersey: "It grieves me to hear that your People have a Prejudice against liberal Education. There is a Spice of this every where. But Liberty has no Enemy more dangerous than such a Prejudice."

It is appalling that, by this standard, liberty today has so many domestic enemies. The practical wisdom necessary to thrive in a free society is the core of a liberal education, which would include training in good judgment, self-knowledge, morality, manners, and self-mastery. From as early on as possible, students should get practice in both giving and judging persuasive argument, by regularly participating in subjuries. As jurors, they would be required to exhibit the demeanor necessary for genuine democratic debate; they could directly learn, in the words of Adam Smith, that "good temper and moderation of contending factions seems to be the most essential circumstance in the publick morals of a free people." According to notes made by Madison, that "good temper and moderation" was achieved at the Constitutional Convention:

**James Madison:** "Disinterestedness & candor demonstrated by mutual concessions, & frequent changes of opinion . . . Few who did not change in the progress of discussions the opinions on important points which they carried into the Convention . . . Few who, at the close of the Convention, were not ready to admit this change as the enlightening effect of the discussions."

By frequently being subjurors, students could gain the habits of civility and sociability that are necessary for being good citizens; they would then be less likely to become slaves to self-destructive emotions or appetites, and more likely to pursue their own happiness without violating the rights of others. In becoming dexterous managers of their own thoughts, passions, and behaviors, they would acquire the private morals to achieve the greatest flourishing of their own lives, the very goal of a free, democratic society.

**Benjamin Rush:** "We do not extol it too highly when we attribute as much to the power of eloquence as to the sword in bringing about the American revolution."

**David Ramsay:** "Eloquence is the child of a free state. In this form of government, as publick measures are determined by a majority of votes, arguments enforced by the arts of persuasion, must evermore be crowned with success: The rising patriot, therefore, who wishes the happiness of his country, will cultivate the art of publick speaking."

Both observations are true enough and necessary for participation in juries, where students could continually gain experience in expressing accurately their own thoughts, feelings, emotions, and aspirations. But they must also learn that this art can be used by the demagogue as well as a statesman, and to recognize irrelevant qualities in judging public figures in democratic societies.

**James Madison:** "It should seem that Caesar excell'd Cicero in the Art of Persuasion."

**John Adams:** "The five Pillars of Aristocracy are Beauty Wealth, Birth, Genius and Virtues. Any one of the three first, can at any time over bear one or both of the two last"

If reason is to rule in judging politicians, the people must be able to see through the language of demagogues, and resist the enticements of "Beauty Wealth, Birth." Students therefore should attain familiarity with the whole phenomenology of human credulity by getting practice in avoiding logical and statistical fallacies; in distinguishing scientists from cranks, and doctors from quacks; in judging the honesty of advertisements; in recognizing auditory, visual, olfactory, and tactile illusions (including the wonderful use magicians make of them); in identifying art forgeries, photographic falsifications, and computer frauds; in connecting some conspiracy theories with motivated believing; in seeing through verbal tricks by which Iago corrupts the character of Othello; in discerning irrational pride, such as that which led to the Hamilton-Burr duel; in learning how propagandists practice their deceptions; in perceiving the dangers of 140 or 280 characters; in analyzing historical claims, such as those who present Jefferson as only a hero, or only a villain; in accurately judging moral character; in studying the long history of fanaticisms, whether the religious (such as the radical parts of Judaism, Christianity, and Islam) or the secular (such as the totalitarian ideologies of fascism and communism). The ability to identify bad reasoning is a required talent in order to fulfill civic duty. Students must understand that *I cannot tell a lie* is as much a fault when listening or reading as it is a virtue when speaking or writing.

**Thomas Jefferson:** "I know no safe depository of the ultimate powers of the society but the people themselves; and if we think them not enlightened enough to exercise their control with a wholesome discretion, the remedy is not to take it from them, but to inform their discretion by education."

If students are to become a "safe depository," they need to internalize the epistemological virtues of a demanding, but practical, ethics of belief, of unbelief, and of suspended belief; their consciousness—in which they live and move and have their being—must become both critical *and* self-critical. Hence honesty, integrity, observation, experiment, and the need for independent verification should be repeatedly instilled until they become ingrained habits, along with the moral courage to recognize bad thinking in themselves, and the moral and perhaps physical courage to speak up when they encounter something contrary to the public good. Students need to be taught how to protect themselves from all threats to their own ability to reason well, both for their own and their country's sake. We don't want them to repeat past moral failures or create new ones. Thus the need to foster individual and social emotions, such as love, care, empathy, and compassion, so that students can better understand themselves, and those who are quite different from themselves. All these efforts will prepare them, both individually and collectively, for the soul-searching job of determining what kind of person, what kind of country, what kind of civilization, is most worthy of their aspirations.

Perhaps the most important virtue is the internal one of being able to recognize the tricks the mind uses to protect against unwanted criticism, whether internal or external. Students must not only avoid the debilitating vice of self-deceit; they must gain the genuine self-mastery needed for the greatest prosperity in a free society. That requires that they learn, in addition to the art of persuading, the art of being persuaded by reason. The latter consists in the ability to recognize or generate sound arguments, combined with the willingness to accept and abide by them, even if that means going against one's initial strong beliefs, or swallowing one's pride, or giving up a cherished goal, or modifying a strong habit, or suffering social embarrassment. Students must not only be taught the weaknesses of the human mind, but also the best workarounds for those weaknesses, and they must be taught so often and so well that excellence in control of their own mind grows into an integral part of their self-identity. They should internalize the deliberative interaction they learn from courts of common reason when they talk to themselves. The aim is to cultivate them to become wise in the exercise of their own political freedom. In contrast, tyrannies depend on ignorance and ubiquitous censorship; they are constantly trying to create a disability to think wisely about moral and political matters, so that the people will never threaten to become a "depository of the ultimate powers of the society."

**Tunis Wortman:** "Introduce the incessant habit of independent reflection, and the establishment of Public Opinion upon a rational and salutary basis will follow as the necessary consequence." "Politics is a subject of universal concern: it relates to objects of public utility. We are equally interested in supporting the genuine principles of Social Security and Happiness. We are entitled to investigate every question which concerns the Public Prosperity. We are equally entitled to communicate the result of our enquiry and deliberation."

America is a be-all-you-can-be civilization, allowing its citizens to be more than they could be under any other form of government. And a universal liberal education should acquaint its citizens with the immense variety of human flourishing, teach the habits of self-knowledge and independent thought needed to choose wisely among that variety, and arouse in them passions to live by those choices. The trouble with learning from just our own experience is that our direct experience is much too limited. We need to learn from the most talented, honest, adventurous, creative, intelligent, sensitive, passionate and extraordinary individuals of all time. Then we will learn about human greatness, about outstanding integrity, about physical and moral courage, about all the virtues that will increase our capacity and relish for excellence in the art of living.

**James Madison:** "To suppose that any form of government will secure liberty or happiness without any virtue in the people, is a chimerical idea"

**John Adams:** "Public Virtue cannot exist in a Nation without private, and public Virtue is the only Foundation of Republics. There must be a possitive Passion for the public good, the public Interest, Honour, Power, and Glory, established in the Minds of the People, or there can be no Republican Government, nor any real Liberty."

We need a professional community trained in science to judge whether something is a genetic disease, or a dinosaur bone, or a supernova; likewise we need a political community trained in the liberal arts and sciences to judge whether we have justice, or equality, or liberty. Today there is much uncertainty about the content of a liberal education, and endless arguments about canons and curricula. Courts of common reason allow the arguments to become evidence-based. When juries have finished their deliberations, the participants could discuss the skills, knowledge, and virtues they needed for that deliberation, and where their own education was admirable or deficient in preparing them for this responsibility. An analysis of all those discussions could determine the core of the curriculum in public schools, so that students would have a superb preparation to fulfill public duties and pursue private happiness.

## THE GOOD FRUIT OF ATHENIAN DEMOCRACY

**Thomas Paine:** "What Athens was in miniature, America will be in magnitude."

**John Adams:** "There is reason to hope for all the equality, all the liberty, and every other good fruit of an Athenian democracy, without any of its ingratitude, levity, convulsions, or factions."

Replacing an elected Congress with a CCR Congress would more than fulfill this hope for a sober Athenian democracy. Ergonomic government would be established, and estrangement between government and the common reason of the people would disappear. But there is at least one good fruit of Athenian democracy that should not be overlooked—the theater. We know Athenian democracy and Athenian theater were born and died together, and that they were thoroughly integrated, an integration which produced one of the greatest sequences of dramatic productions (over a thousand) that the world has ever known. We know this even though the surviving sample of thirty-odd plays is tiny. We also know this sequence was the result of a competition in a yearly festival, in which decisions about the winners were made by ordinary citizens who held one-year political terms.

Let our thought experiment include, as part of Project Athena, a yearly *Festival America*—say, five days long—in which American values and culture are celebrated in ritual, music, dance, art, and drama. The Festival, we may suppose, will be the finals in a nationwide competition for the best dramatic productions. Its organization will be such as to emphasize the diversity of American talent and sensibility. It could include comedies in which we laugh at our pretensions and stupidities; tragedies where the virtues and faults of American character are disclosed; and histories where persons and events in our past are celebrated or condemned. Of course, it would be a juried arts festival, where the juries would be "in miniature, an exact portrait of the people at large," and the plays would have been chosen through democratic evolutionary designs, so that successful playwrights would have many opportunities for rewrites.

Festival America could end on the Forth of July. The civic art could become part of school curricula in order to unite and inspire the next generation in ways that perhaps nothing else could. Some plays students would no doubt remember their entire lives, thereby becoming new American classics. Human beings apparently present us with a reality such that literal speech about them misses something essential; they seem to possess both "real" and "imaginary" components. Festival America would allow the American people to forge a new integrity in their lives by combining their moral, economic, and political perceptions in an external world of experience, with their aesthetic, ideal, and aspirational perceptions in an internal world of reflection. This would create, as it were, a cultural double helix, that would reveal the foundational DNA of American civilization. No entirely nonpoetic, nonfictional, nonmythical account of human experience seems to capture the full reality of life as it is actually lived. The Festival could generate the right myths, music, rituals, and aspirations for life in a free society. For the first time in its history, America's fractured soul could be made whole. We have copied the ancient Greeks by reintroducing the Olympics, an introduction that has regularly produced incomparable athletic achievement. It is surely not beyond the ingenuity of Americans to copy, adapt, and improve upon the Athenian Festival so that it regularly produces incomparable dramatic works in the pursuit of public happiness.

**John Jay:** "While reason retains her rule, while men are as ready to receive as to give advice, and as willing to be convinced themselves as to convince others, there are few political evils from which a free and enlightened people cannot deliver themselves."

**James Madison:** "So strong is this propensity of mankind to fall into mutual animosities, that where no substantial occasion presents itself, the most frivolous and fanciful distinctions have been sufficient to kindle their unfriendly passions, and excite their most violent conflicts."

The aim of Project Athena is to make Jay's observation the reality in courts of common reason, but achieving that reality must face the difficulty in Madison's insight. Perhaps juried democracy will sometimes arouse significant factions that didn't exist before. Emotions contrary to reason are a constant danger to human happiness and, to defeat those emotions, the power of art must be used to enflame counter passions in the cause of humanity, such as the love of truth and the yearning for justice. Of course, artists can use their talent in the service of inhumanity; the art of Leni Riefenstahl, who lent her talents to Hitler, and Sergei Eisenstein, who lent his to Stalin, come to mind. The power of art, like the power of technology, can be misused.

**John Adams:** "Every one of the fine Arts from the earliest times has been inlisted in the service of Superstition and

Despotism."

In Festival America it would be the people's responsibility to deliberate and then distinguish such art from that which best contributes to the public good. There would be no hint whatsoever of censorship here; free persons could enjoy any kind of art they wish; Adams includes "Homer and Milton Phidias and Raphael" among those that support "the grossest Fictions." But it doesn't follow that any art or music that pleases an individual, even those exhibiting transcendent talent, will be seen by a soul-searching people as the most appropriate for free persons in a free society to choose for their own moral and political enhancement. Rather, the people could choose art and music for Festival America which will strengthen those emotions that their common reason approves, and which will protect them from the poetic injustice of any inhumane art that might undermine their character, their liberties, their happiness.

**The Bostonian (pseudonym):** "A virtuous Theatre, combining every energy that can awake and excite [man's] ambition, will enlarge his views, correct his manners, and exalt his aims, to every great and noble pursuit, within the compass of human excellence!"

**James Sullivan (1795):** Sullivan argued that, to eradicate slavery, the children of black slaves must be educated at the same schools and in the same manner as white children. He then says: "There is an objection to this, which embraces all my feelings; that is, that it will tend to a mixture of blood, which I now abhor; but yet, as I feel, I fear that I am not a pure Republican, delighting in the equal rights of the human race."

In such cases as Sullivan's, where feelings prevent individuals from "delighting in the equal rights of the human race," might it not be prudent, might it not be necessary, to employ the power of a "virtuous Theatre" to modify those feelings, at least far enough so that they lose their power to corrupt thought or action? Let us then suppose that the winning plays in Festival America would routinely be seen by current or future juries, as part of their preparation to make political decisions. Metajuries would decide which plays, if any, would be chosen for each political issue. By integrating these plays into their jury duties, jurors would be in a better position to make their fateful judgments wisely, since their imagination, empathy and self-insight would be strengthened and enlarged by art.

**Thomas Jefferson:** "A lively and lasting sense of filial duty is more effectually impressed on the mind of a son or daughter by reading King Lear, than by all the dry volumes of ethics and divinity that ever were written."

So imagine in a given year that one category in Festival America consisted of three plays—a tragedy, comedy, and history—dealing with problems of racism in America. Now when any Court of Common Reason considered a topic involving these problems, they would not deliberate and vote without seeing and discussing the winning plays. This practice would exploit the power of art to increase the likelihood of informed and humane judgments by members of the jury. Remember that even clear and valid arguments may be incapable of changing beliefs that are emotionally charged, such as those that are motivated, or based on hatred, prejudices, bigotry, and self-deceit. Since difficulties concerning relations between the races can nowhere be solved but in the minds, hearts, and wills of the people, would it not be advantageous to construct a morally therapeutic procedure in which art, chosen by the people themselves, informs their deliberations, and perhaps transforms their minds, hearts, and wills? The young must be prepared to be juried democrats by a education that aims at a tripartite integrity, consisting of all the intellectual, emotional, and volitional elements that make up their character.

**Noah Webster:** Webster, one of the founders of Amherst Academy (now Amherst College), said the Academy's duty to its students is "to enlighten their minds; to exalt their character; and to teach them the way to happiness and glory."

**Thomas Jefferson:** "The first elements of morality" shows young people "how to work out their own greatest happiness."

Webster and Jefferson are here presupposing that free persons, competently educated, are the foundation of moral and political progress; that Americans should constantly try to improve their own pursuits of Cicero's "higher happiness," to the benefit of themselves, their country, and their posterity. Invigorating this virtue, at once both private and public, is the *raison d'etre* of Festival America.

**John Adams (May 1776):** "When I consider the great Events which are passed, and those greater which are rapidly advancing, and that I may have been instrumental of touching some Springs, and turning small Wheels, which have had and will have such Effects, I feel an Awe upon my Mind, which is not easily described."

The experience of deciding great public issues in Courts of Common Reason; of sometimes beginning with a tense division and, after deliberations and theater, ending with a virtual consensus (forming a "more perfect Union"); and then celebrating such deliberations in Festival America could all combine to instill this revolutionary awe in the American people. Many jurors might see their duty as an education that makes them better human beings—as a good in itself—and thus they would be willing, even eager, to serve, despite the strenuous and at times upsetting quality of that participation. They would be in "the pursuit of happiness, striving even to an Agony," to use a phrase from a 1669 British book.

Festival America might include a category for students, where they could submit short stories, plays, songs, even political games, and the winners could be considered by local or state Courts of Common Reason for inclusion in future curricula. Students might also choose the fifty works of art to be learned from among the hundreds that historians of art might deem appropriate, or the three proofs of the Pythagorean Theorem that students judge best combine simplicity, clarity, and the beautiful from the many scores that have been devised. Perhaps a national advisory jury of, say, eight-graders, could pick a superb collection of short stories, that would better instill a love of learning in themselves than adults ever could. Again, might not the job, say, of picking the best plays about bullying make it less likely that they would become bullies? It is easy to think of other problems, such as drugs, sexism, racism, violence, alienation, suicide, where knowing the considered judgment of students might be necessary to solve their social problems.

The ultimate goal is to infuse in students the practical wisdom to felicitously conduct their lives; and by striving to answer questions about the education of the next generation of students, they will learn something about how to conduct their own future education—what maxims to follow, what books to read, what videos to see, what computer games to play, and what social or life experiences to seek out. If we made the utmost use of the ability of students to teach other students, we might be able to greatly increase the efficiency and quality of education. If we truly love our children, if we want them to flourish as free persons in a free society, they must become responsible for their own education, and we must, as early and as often as is reasonable, educate them to educate themselves for their coming adult life in a juried democracy,  Here the proper procedure is to experiment, experiment, experiment.

To be civilized requires the arousal and exercise of refined emotions, including the moral (such as passions of love and empathy), the political (such as passions for liberty and justice), and the epistemological (such as passions for truth and reason).  The arts are indispensable elements in refining that arousal and exercise.  Just as our bodily life is less likely to be healthy if we do not fully integrate science into our medicine, so our civic life is less likely to be happy if we do not fully integrate the arts into our politics.

Democratic autonomy cannot be achieved without deliberative soul-searching among the people; it is the foundation of political excellence in a free society; in eighteenth-century language, it is the foundation of public happiness.  Project Athena gives us an opportunity to create a new class of systemic solutions to social problems, true moral and political antibiotics, not the mere antiseptics that have been used so far.  In the kind of art they choose, in the way they conduct their deliberations, the people could use their common reason to overcome the moral and political faults they see in themselves, and by this self-examination of their national character, they could collectively become their own philosopher-king.

**Gouverneur Morris:** "The people are the King."

**John Adams:** "Know thyself is as useful a precept to nations as to men."

**James Wilson:** "A nation ought to know itself. It ought to form a just estimate of its own situation, both with regard to itself and to its neighbours. It ought to learn the excellencies, and the blemishes likewise of its own constitution. It ought to review the instances in which it has already attained, and it ought to ascertain those in which it falls short of, a practicable degree of perfection."

These wise sentiments have been, and will remain, empty verbal pieties until courts of common reason or their equivalent are established. Courts of Common Reason are the brain scanners of the body politic, allowing the people to create a genuine *politics of self-knowledge,* though which they can know their own minds, feelings, and humanity. For the first time in our history, an authoritative articulation of the American dream would be possible. Such an endeavor requires an investigative spirit that maintains a continuing and rigorous examination by the people of the philosophic basis of their own government and society, so as to be sure it is worthy of their belief, their commitment, their aspirations. America is Delphic-based civilization; without a *know thyself* base, the American Revolution dissolves into thin air.

**John Adams:** "Men should endeavor at a balance of affections and appetites, under the monarchy of reason and conscience, within, as well as at a balance of power without."

By nature, we are born with great capacities but are dependent, ignorant, and possess just animal talents; through a liberal arts and sciences education, *inculcated to become second nature,* we can exploit all our human capacities until we are reborn with the autonomy, knowledge, and aptitude to master the art of living well today, and even better tomorrow.

## THE ARTS AND MORAL FREEDOM

In order to achieve that wonderful goal, it is necessary to discuss *moral freedom*. It is seldom talked about today in public discourse, so let's try to learn from the American revolutionaries.

**Joel Barlow (July 4, 1787):** "We have contended with the most powerful nation and subdued the bravest and best appointed armies; but now we have to contend with *ourselves*, and encounter passions and prejudices more powerful than armies and more dangerous to peace."

**Gad Hitchcock:** "Liberty is the spirit and genius of the sacred writings; the great thing aimed at in them, is to make men free from sin; to deliver them out of bondage to their lusts, and procure and establish the moral freedom of their minds."

**Samuel West:** "When a man goes beyond, or contrary to the law of nature and reason, he becomes the slave of base passions, and vile lusts, he introduces confusion and disorder into society, and brings misery and destruction upon himself. This therefore cannot be called a state of freedom, but a state of the vilest slavery, and the most dreadful bondage: The servants of sin and corruption are subjected to the worst kind of tyranny in the universe. Hence we conclude, that where licentiousness begins, liberty ends."

**Phillips Payson:** "If the reason of the mind, man's immediate rule of conduct, is in bondage to corruption, he is verily the worst of slaves."

**John Mellen:** "But he is the man of freedom, in the most noble sense, who has the command of himself, who can rule his own spirit, command his own passions and appetites, keep under his body, and make reason the rule of his conduct — who fears God and walks uprightly, and orders his conversation aright. He that is master of himself is King. Bloody heroes conquer *others,* he subdues *himself,* a world greater and better than that without him. To take a city is now-a-days, a trifle. He that gets possession of the *world within* is greater than *Alexander.* For though a man may acquire universal empire, he may yet die a slave to his vanity and lust."

*Moral freedom* means the habitual exercise of reason in the pursuit of either private or public happiness. If we wish to be true and complete American revolutionaries, we must cultivate both moral and political freedom. In a politically free country the external restrictions on an individual's pursuit of happiness exist only to maintain or increase that freedom. Examples might include: laws forbidding the power to legally contract oneself into slavery, or laws prohibiting the choice to not educate one's own children, or laws in the United States denying the freedom to drive on the left side of the road. In a morally free person, the internal obstacles must be directed by a rational conscience to also increase freedom. Both kinds of freedom are subject to degrees and both are complex; one can be politically free in one way but not another, one can be morally free in one way but not another. If a person is born free in the political sense of freedom, it is a gift of society. Jefferson received the gift; his slaves did not. However, a person cannot be born free in the moral sense. In that meaning we are all born dependent and ignorant, this freedom is not a gift of society, but an achievement of the individual. Jame Hubbard achieved moral freedom when he ran away, fulfilling a *duty* he had from the Declaration, whereas Jefferson was not morally free to fulfill his duty from the same source.

**John Adams (1765):** "Let us see delineated before us, the true map of man. Let us hear the dignity of his nature, and the noble rank he holds among the works of God! that consenting to slavery is a sacrilegious breach of trust, as offensive in the sight of God, as it is derogatory from our own honor or interest or happiness."

The goal of the American Revolution is to create the best possible political and social conditions favorable to the development of a rational conscience. Just as our common reason should make us wise masters of our common government, so our individual reason should make us wise masters in governing ourselves, allowing each person to conquer the "world within." American happiness requires that we relentlessly oppose any self-deceit, rationalizations, prejudices, feelings, or emotions that might stand in the way of moral freedom. The stirring words marking the end of bodily slavery—Free at last! Free at last! Thank God Almighty, we are free at last!—will be equally appropriate when moral slavery ends. We need a new class of abolitionist leaders: journalists who will not equivocate, excuse, or retreat, orators who will be heard, artists who will enlighten, educators who will teach, politicians who will act, until our civilization becomes, and forever remains, nothing but the offspring of the moral freedom of the American people.

Let us call any psychic habit or activity that undermines moral freedom a *corruption of consciousness*. The mighty intellect of Jefferson was "verily the worst of slaves" when he tried to reason about blacks or himself. For him, the "people in mass . . . are inherently independent of all but moral law," yet for him also, the political government of Virginia, the petty government of Monticello, and the moral government of Thomas Jefferson were above that law. His licentious lust for power over others led him to defend hereditary slavery: arguing that the power "to regulate the condition of the different descriptions of men composing a State" is "the exclusive right of every State." (Douglass: "While there remains such an idea as the right of each State to control its own local affairs . . . no general assertion of human rights can be of any practical value. . . . All that is necessary to be done is to make the government consistent with itself, and render the rights of the States compatible with the sacred rights of human nature.") Since hereditary slavery is contrary to the "sacred rights" expressed by "Laws of Nature and of Nature's God," the governments of Virginia and Monticello are crimes against humanity. It is almost impossible to study Jefferson and not be jealous of his colossal and wide-ranging talents; but who would want such talents, or the fame they brought, if the price were the depravity in one's character comparable to Jefferson's self-deceit? We miss half of the meaning of the American Revolution, as most accounts of it do, if we limit our attention to avoiding external slavery and securing its extreme opposite called political freedom; for the other half is avoiding the internal slavery of a corrupt consciousness and securing its extreme opposite called moral freedom.

Let us reflect on the words of the art critic Bernard Berenson: "All of the arts, poetry, music, ritual, the visual arts, the theatre, must singly and together create the most comprehensive art of all, a humanized society, and its masterpiece, the free man; free within and free without." Since the American perfectionist ethos aims to make every citizen a "masterpiece," the arts chosen by the people—for their own protection against corrupt consciousness—must become an intrinsic part of our political experience. Their potentially great humane effect should not be left to chance.

Jefferson's and Madison's liberal education combined with their transcendent genius did not prevent them from being traitors to humanity. This catastrophic failure was fostered by a schooling that did not instill the virtues of intellectual integrity, moral courage, and social empathy. In spite of appearances, their education was not fully liberal. They became their own jailers by creating a psychic confinement imperceivable to their mind's eye; escape becomes unnecessary, indeed unthinkable. In 1776 Jefferson's "all Men are created equal" put the final nail in Aristotle's claim that "from the hour of their birth, some are marked out for subjection, others for rule." In 1785 Madison presented a slavery bill (composed by Jefferson) to the Virginia legislature. It was rejected by the slaveholding legislators as too cruel. But Madison, like Jefferson, did not think of himself as advocate of tyranny. Just three years later Madison said, "I profess myself to have had a uniform zeal for a republican government."

**James Madison:** "We all know that . . . conscience itself may be deluded; may be misled, by an unconscious bias, into acts which an enlightened conscience would forbid."

An anthropology of human felicity must pay as much attention to the moral ecology of the mind as it does to the political ecology of society. No country is securely safe or free if ignorance, prejudices, and passions make its leaders slaves to themselves. Hence self-insight, intellectual integrity, moral courage, and social empathy must be as strongly instilled in the education of citizens, as physical courage is in the training of Marines. We cannot be the land of the free because we are the home of the brave, unless that bravery also be exhibited against personal and social self-deception. What is the use of having political freedom of conscience if you are not morally free enough to exercise that right? Eighteenth-century America lacked the kind of poetry, fiction, and drama that would expose and counteract corruptions of consciousness. A large literature containing sound and often eloquent arguments against racism and slavery then existed; yet arguments were not adequate to penetrate the self-deceptive mind. In 1881, Douglass, himself a runaway slave, wrote: "In the midst of these fugitive slave troubles came the book known as *Uncle Tom's Cabin*, a work of marvelous depth and power. Nothing could have better united the moral and human requirements of the hour. Its effect was amazing, instantaneous, and universal." Perhaps it is not too much to say that had the eighteenth century been blessed with a Stowe, she might have helped prevent, rather than help start, the Civil War.

**Thomas Jefferson:** "I have sworn upon the altar of God, eternal hostility against every form of tyranny over the mind of man."

Yet Jefferson never showed any hostility to the artful lies, the falsehoods, the specious reasoning, that tyrannized his own thinking on blacks, because he himself was in a "dreadful bondage." That corrupt consciousness could be found in various degrees and various ways in the minds of many ordinary people as well as political leaders. Hence the road to America's coming calamity was not blocked either by political leaders, or by revolts of the people. Self-deceivers did not see what they did not want to see (the contradiction between their practice and their principles), did not feel what they did not want to feel (sympathy for the plight of the slave), and did not act where they did not want to act (by giving blacks a liberal education). Character counts in perfecting the pursuit of happiness.

When Athenian democracy was young, the Greeks, although badly outnumbered, defeated the Persians at Marathon (490 B.C.), at Salamis (480), at Plataea (479). In 472 Aeschylus won first prize in the Athenian Festival for his play *The Persians*. In it, the Persian Queen asks who is king of the Athenians. The answer: "Of no man are they called the slaves or vassals." For the Athenian audience where many, like Aeschylus himself, were veterans, and where all had relatives, friends, or associates who died fighting the Persians, this may have been the most soul-stirring line of poetry they had ever heard; for it meant their democratic valor in war had protected Athens from becoming a new Miletus (which had been destroyed in 494 after the Greek city revolted against Persian subjugation); it meant that they would never have to prostrate themselves, as the Persians had to do, before any monarch; it meant that they were free of all political oppressors, whether foreign or domestic; it meant their unique democratic freedom would henceforth *define* them as Athenians; it meant that the flourishing of that freedom would honor, as nothing else could, those who fought and died for Athens.

By the twenty-first century, Philadelphia freedom has perfected Athenian freedom in many, many ways, but it has done little to protect the people and its leaders from the idols of the mind that pervert human reason. If Project Athena were successful, Americans would forge within themselves a new civic character, by developing a scrupulous integrity, an unyielding moral courage, an unfailing empathy, and a common reason that joined together could subdue those qualities of mind that compromise the pursuit of excellence in the art of living. After the display of unprecedented honesty, tenacity, and democratic valor in wrenching, soul-searching defeats of these enemies within—moral equivalents of Marathon, Salamis, and Plataea—perhaps a play in Festival America would identify these new, new Americans by the phrase: "Of no corruption of consciousness are they called the slaves or vassals."

## AMERICA'S ADDICTION TO PARTIES

Athenian democracy existed for centuries without parties. Hence, unlike individual disagreements within human societies, parties are not built into human nature. Today, unfortunately, they are ubiquitous in democratic governments.

**Thomas Day:** "Among those means, which are calculated to destroy a free government, none will be found more efficient than PARTY SPIRIT. It has long been said, and sanctioned by the authority of Heaven, that, 'A HOUSE DIVIDED AGAINST ITSELF CANNOT STAND.' "

**George Clinton:** "Beware of the spirit of party: it may dissolve your union, dismember your empire, and render you the sport of ambition, and the cause of your own destruction."

**John Adams:** "While all other Sciences have advanced, that of Government is at a stand; little better understood; little better practiced now than 3 or 4 thousand Years ago. What is the Reason? I say Parties and Factions will not suffer, or permit Improvements to be made." "There is nothing which I dread so much as a division of the republic into two great parties, each arranged under its leader, and concerting measures in opposition to each other. This, in my humble apprehension, is to be dreaded as the greatest political evil under our Constitution [that is, the Massachusetts Constitution of 1780]."

**George Washington:** "[The Spirit of Party] exists under different shapes in all Governments, more or less stifled, controuled, or repressed; but, in those of the popular form it is seen in its greatest rankness and is truly their worst enemy."

**Thomas Jefferson:** "I never submitted the whole system of my opinions to the creed of any party of men whatever in religion, in philosophy, in politics, or in any thing else where I was capable of thinking for myself. Such an addiction is the last degradation of a free and moral agent."

Again, we see that the politics the founding generation bequeathed to us was not the politics they aspired to. When they formed parties they were putting their country—and their own moral character—at risk. Jefferson's fine words, for instance, did not prevent him from becoming addicted to a party of his own creation, whose aim was to create a racist groupthink to protect slavery; he truly embodied "the last degradation of a free and moral agent."

**John Adams:** "There is nothing in the science of human nature, more curious, or that deserves a critical attention from every order of men, so much, as that principle, which moral writers have distinguished by the name of *self-deceit*. This principle is the spurious offspring of *self-love*; and is perhaps the source of far the greatest, and worst part of the vices and calamities among mankind."

Surprisingly, Adams himself succumbed to this mental vice, although to a lesser extent than Jefferson. Here is a man who is admirable in so many ways—he is philosophically insightful, he demonstrated both moral and physical courage on numerous occasions, it is easy to find him lovable—even this great man indulges in gross and prolonged self-deceit. In 1776 he was a member of the committee that produced the Declaration of Independence. Yet he was incapable of seeing blacks as he saw whites, as bearers of God-given natural rights that no human can ever justly violate; much less did he see the moral collapse of his own character when, after the revolutionary war, he said that his philosophical opposition to the slave trade would not prevent him from doing everything he could to get former slaves returned that were in British hands. Five years before he died (in 1826) he wrote to Jefferson: "I have been so terrified with this Phenomenon [slavery] that I constantly said in former times to the Southern Gentlemen, I cannot comprehend this object; I must leave it to you. I will vote for forceing no measure against your judgements." Translation: In my politics, the slave party, although not mine, trumps the Declaration of Independence to which I pledged my life, my fortune, and my sacred honor.

Nothing we have learned about parties since the eighteenth century relieves our existential worries about how they undermine truth, integrity, patriotism, and moral freedom. Yet we virtually completely ignore this indisputable lesson of history, even though our technology makes their risks and corruptions substantially greater. A delusion is haunting America, the delusion that a *democratic* republic can be administered by parties, who in fact are America's "worst enemy" and "greatest political evil." They are the principal creators and supporters of systemic divisions among the American people and routinely undermine the rule of law (while boasting that they support it).

**John Adams:** "The interest of the people is one thing—it is the public interest; and where the public interest governs, it is a government of laws, and not of men; the interest of a king, or of a party is another thing—it is a private interest; and where private interest governs, it is a government of men, not of laws."

The interest of a party is the interest of its base. Hence presidents are often ready to swear allegiance to a Constitution that begins "WE THE PEOPLE OF THE UNITED STATES, in Order to form a more perfect Union"; yet they spend much of their time forming a more imperfect union. The Founders who believed they were devoted to a democratic republic practiced or tolerated slavery. The evil of parties in the twenty-first century is different from the absolute evil of slavery; nevertheless, parties are as convenient for politicians today as slavery was then for plantation owners, and they now rival eighteenth-century slavery in their capacity to corrupt public reason and thus the moral freedom of the people that is necessary to create a government solely devoted to the common good.

Again, the Preamble of the Constitution tells us that one of its purposes is to "establish Justice." Yet decade after decade, parties tolerate vastly different treatment courts give the rich and the poor which means, of course, that they have not yet established justice. Our party leaders entertain the self-deceitful belief—a "spurious offspring of *self-love*"—that their earnest pledges to uphold the Constitution are genuine. They run an oligarchic republic, while what made the ideals of the American Revolution uniquely valuable to humanity was the revolutionary aspiration to make the United States into a democratic republic, where justice is defined by the people and secured by juries.

**James Madison:** "It is . . . certain, that there are various ways in which the rich may oppress the poor; in which property may oppress liberty; and that the world is filled with examples. It is necessary that the poor should have a defence against the danger."

**John Adams:** Poor people have rights "undoubtedly, antecedent to all earthly government,—*Rights* that cannot be repealed or restrained by human laws—*Rights* derived from the great Legislator of the universe."

The success of Project Athena would allow rights for the poor to be identified and established. Thus each year courts of common reason could compare a random sample of the sort of justice that the richest defendants receive, compared with that of the poorest. Any differences that violated the American people's deliberative sense of equal justice would have to be remedied; Our courts might finally stop grossly violating the Magna Carta (1215): "To none will we sell . . . right or justice." This might be achieved by having the government supply judges, prosecutors, *and* defense lawyers, each being chosen randomly for any given trial. Further, metajuries could determine what other groups may be at greater risk of injustice, and hence should get special attention from a Court of Common Reason. Examples might be native Americans, the homeless, prisoners, sex workers, foreigners, immigrants, the mentally ill, the physically handicapped, children, racial or sexual minorities, "white trash," workers in a dying industry, and even the rich, if metajuries rule that their property is being subject to arbitrary or unjust taxation. After extensive use of hybrid juries, half from a vulnerable group, half from the general population, these injustices could be identified and corrected by Courts of Common Reason. It would include deliberating the plight of each vulnerable group after considering their history and present situation, attending winning plays about them from Festival America, again deliberating, and then deciding. Our politicians are morally blind to the obvious: That the party system with elections cannot consistently form a more perfect union, or establish justice. That can only be achieved by "WE THE PEOPLE," and *we the people* at their best. And that best is what Project Athena is seeking to find and make sovereign.

**Anonymous:** "Whoever frames to himself an idea of a perfect republican government must necessarily consider the inhabitants in the highest stages of refinement, possessing the moral and social virtues in the highest perfection."

"Anonymous" shows that it was then known that

perfectionist thought experiments were as indispensable to understand republican politics as they were (and are) to understand physics. One of these republican perfections is universal education in *self-critical thinking*, which was described by John Mason, whose 1745 book *Self-Knowledge* was widely read in eighteenth-century America: "Before we let our Thoughts judge of Things, we must set Reason to judge our Thoughts; for they are not always in a proper Condition to execute that Office. We do not believe the Character which a Man gives us of another, unless we have a good Opinion of his own; so neither should we believe the Verdict which the Mind pronounces, till we first examine whether it be impartial and unbiased; whether it be in a proper Temper to judge, and have proper Lights to judge by. The Want of this previous *Act of Self Judgment*, is the Cause of much Self Deception and false Judgment."

The habitual exercise of such self-critical thinking continues to be one of the most important parts of science. In his 1974 commencement address at the California Institute of Technology, Richard Feynman said: "But this long history of learning how to not fool ourselves—of having utter scientific integrity—is, I'm sorry to say, something that we haven't specifically included in any particular course that I know of. We just hope you've caught on by osmosis. The first principle is that you must not fool yourself—and you are the easiest person to fool. . . . I'm talking about a specific, extra type of integrity that is not lying, but bending over backwards to show how you're maybe wrong, that you ought to have when acting as a scientist" or, we may add, when acting as a citizen in a democratic republic.

Party politics is constantly at war with a bend-over-backwards integrity. If successful, Project Athena will not only destroy toxic parties, but will infuse into Americans a recognition of the vast dangers of self-deception. It is a monumental educational challenge, though seldom recognized, to figure out how to instill a life-long habit in children and young people of using their reason to decide correctly whether their own minds, and those of others, "be in a proper Temper to judge, and have proper Lights to judge by." And Project Athena can have no more difficult task than to structure courts of common reason so that the probability their conclusions is a product of social self-deception, is always at a practical minimum. Success here is required to produce that moral and political excellence which is the aspiration of any juried democracy,

Without a soaring effort comparable to that put into the development of the airplane or the computer—both of which were called foolish, inefficient, utopian fantasies—we cannot with plausibility declare that Project Athena must be a failure in practice. The initial failure, but the ultimate stunning success, of the Hubble telescope—a "big science" project—was possible because the promise of a revolution in our knowledge of the heavens, or of our power to get there, lured or generated the magnificent talent necessary to produce that success. Similarly, Project Athena—a "big political science" project—may seem impractical, but impractical compared to what? Not to governments around the world—including our own—that threaten humanity's existence. If it fails, it would be a noble failure since it might lure or generate the talent necessary for glorious triumph, because it promises to revolutionize our knowledge of ourselves, and our power to control ourselves, thereby creating an unprecedented perfection in self-government.

**Thomas Paine:** "There is existing in man, a mass of sense lying in a dormant state, and which, unless something excites it to action, will descend with him, in that condition, to the grave. As it is to the advantage of society that the whole of its faculties should be employed, the construction of government ought to be such as to bring forward, by a quiet and regular operation, all that extent of capacity which never fails to appear in revolutions."

**Alexander Hamilton:** "Great revolutions . . . serve to bring to light talents and virtues which might otherwise have languished in obscurity or only shot forth a few scattered and wandering rays."

**David Ramsay:** The American Revolution "gave occasion for the display of abilities which, but for that event, would have been lost to the world. . . . It seemed as if the war not only required, but created talents. Men whose minds were warmed with the love of liberty, and whose abilities were improved by daily exercise, and sharpened with a laudable ambition to serve their distressed country, spoke, wrote, and acted, with an energy far surpassing all expectations which could be reasonably founded on their previous acquirements."

Almost by definition, the birth of a revolution brings forth more doubters than believers; otherwise, it is not revolutionary.. Over the  years I worked on Project Athena, I also had lots of doubts; but they were gradually overcome when I learned that the political geniuses from eighteenth-century America believed a juried democracy was the perfect government for humanity, but that it was out of their reach in practice. I was no match for their intellects or talents, but I was sure I could not claim it was beyond *our* practical reach. I did not want to bet against the American people; nor did I want to be the political equivalent of those who opposed Project Apollo because they lacked the knowledge or imagination or self-insight to understand that the issue could only be solved by experiments, not by present doubts. So I asked: Could Americans scale up the good fruit of Athenian democracy while replacing the bad fruit—such as slavery or its treatment of women—with the best fruit that our knowledge and creativity could muster? Without quite realizing it, I slowly adopted the revolutionary exuberance of the Founders for juried democracy. It is a melancholy reflection that our political leaders do not equal the intellectual excellence of our Founders, even with a population a hundred times larger, and one where blacks, women, and native Americans can take part. If we want transcendent talent in politics it must be based on revolutionary philosophy. Aristotle thought men were political animals, the Founders that humans were *revolutionary* political animals. And what would be more revolutionary for us than for Project Athena to demonstrate, by experiment after experiment after experiment, that the American people can solve their inevitable political differences without force, fraud, self-deception, or the evils of parties? Four hundred years ago, Francis Bacon said: "Marvel not if [common people] speak truer than the great, for they speak safer." Every patriot of America, every friend of humanity, would want that vast quarry of truth to be mined to its greatest achievable purity.

## UNDERSTANDING OUR CONSTITUTION

The central philosophical presupposition of the American Revolution is that dignity is innate in human nature and that from this assumption certain political principles follow. But what is dignity? Imagine playing Tag. Here one person is "It" and must chase others; if he or she can tag one of the others, the tagged person becomes "It". Now "Itness" is not a natural property of humans, it has only *game-theoretic existence*, like being "Vulnerable" in bridge, or being "Quarterback" in football. If we play the moral and political game of Dignity, then each person is a bearer of rights, which we must respect; nobody is a nobody. That respect does not necessarily imply esteem. Wicked people are human. But just as the game of Tag requires that we respond to a person who is "It" by running away, so the game of American politics requires that we respond to persons by respecting their dignity. In this *game-theoretic* approach, the property of having "dignity" requires no more reality than the property of being "It". So skeptics may say with David Hume: "Life is like a game: One may choose the game." However, the ethos of the American Revolution does not allow any possible choice; rather, it requires that we choose only the moral and political games that presuppose the dignity of each human being.

**John Adams:** A proper constitution "introduces knowledge among the People, and inspires them with a conscious dignity, becoming Freemen. A general emulation takes place, which causes good humour, sociability, good manners, and good morals to be general."

According to animal psychologists, individual animals—such as dogs, lions, otters, or chimpanzees—require specific kinds of play in order to become, and to continue as excellent examples of their species. Without them, they  become stunted in their psychic growth. Humans, likewise, are similarly affected if, as children, for example, they are deprived of their language games. America is an experiment which seeks to demonstrate that humans—*all* humans—prosper best when they are in a political community which has the Dignity game as its basis. That game requires that each individual be endowed with a freedom and equality that is protected by a justice defined by the common reason of American society. The Revolution's leaders were rightly proud of discovering this game as the best possible one for humans to become excellent examples of human nature at its flourishing best.

**Zephaniah Swift (1792):** "Uncontrouled power corrupts both the heart, and understanding, and tends to eradicate every laudable principle."

Drunk with power, most of the Revolution's leaders proved intransigent on slavery even when directly confronted. For instance, Edward Coles asked Jefferson to "put into complete practice those hallowed principles contained in that renowned Declaration." To Madison, he said: "It seems to me repugnant to the distinctive & characteristic traits of your character—nay pardon me for saying, it would be a blot and stigma on your otherwise spotless escutcheon, not to restore your slaves that liberty & those rights which you have been through life so zealous and able a champion." Here then is the origin of American racism: Some white humans, with a conscience that continually bothers them, downgrade the humanity of blacks until black slavery is transformed from an abomination to a positive good for both white society *and* blacks. The psychic reward of such downgrading is a quiet conscience: "I can be *both* a good person and a slaveholder." This motivated falsehood, beginning with an hypocrisy that eventually becomes self-deceit, creates a stench about Jefferson and Madison that cannot be sweetened by all the perfumes of their intellectual and political genius.

**John Adams:** "There is no special providence for Americans, and their nature is the same with that of others." "We may boast that We are the chosen People; We may even thank God that We are not like other Men. But after all it will be but flattery, and the delusion, the Self-deceit of the Pharisee."

These sentiments against American hubris and self-deception are as wise today as when they were written. There is no "manifest destiny" that gives the United States—much less its leaders—a monopoly on democratic leadership. While America is in a *dreamless* sleep, a juried democracy might create a more perfect European Union, or a better Norway, Brazil, India, Singapore, Republic of South Africa; or even a better China, Russia, Iran, and North Korea. It would certainly be an interesting experiment to see if the Israelis and Palestinians, without the burden of party leaders, could solve their problems using hybrid juries to talk directly to one another. In the twenty-first century, the ease of communication and travel forces us to recognize that even very distant humans are entangled with one another in many and complex ways, and that each government has a duty to help other governments when it can in the cause of humanity. In early America it was common for Northerners to consider slavery a distant Southern problem, when it was also their problem, as the Civil war ultimately demonstrated. Our human earth is now obviously entangled; climate collapse, nuclear war, and pandemics make clear the existence of any government that does not treat humans with dignity may also become America's problem. Yet if America sleeps, Project Athena might be embraced by another country, and it might prove that the best outcome is a global federalism of juried democracies, where hybrid juries are the uniform mechanism for conflict resolution among all governments. Anywhere on the face of the earth where experiments are being made to establish juried democracies in the cause of humanity, there is the American Revolution, even if no Americans have any part in it.

Nevertheless, given its history and resources, the United States is in the best position to lead the world in such a revolution. A juried democracy is both a renaissance of the spirit of 1776, and a reformation of our present practice. Undertaking to new model our country in that spirit is not without its hazards, yet the substantial risk of complete failure did not prevent the creation and adoption of the Constitution of 1787.

Our situation brings to mind the words of John Milton (1644): "I cannot praise a fugitive and cloister'd vertue, unexercis'd & unbreath'd, that never sallies out and sees her adversary, but slinks out of the race, where that immortall garland is to be run for, not without dust and heat. Assuredly we bring not innocence into the world, we bring impurity much rather: that which purifies us is triall, and triall is by what is contrary." Our government should uncloister the "vertue" of the American people, they ought to be purified by the "triall" of contraries in Courts of Common Reason, purified by being confronted, again and again, with America's most excruciatingly difficult moral and political problems. Their deliberations are the democratic process; no democratic republic can usurp their responsibility, their freedom, or their autonomy, by making hard and fateful decisions for them. Or do we slink out of the race for the "immortall garland" of unprecedented excellence in the pursuit of democratic perfection because we fear what the people might decide, after soul-searching reflection, agonistic deliberation, and the humanizing effect of the arts? Is a cloistered virtue in the cause of humanity the best we Americans will ever achieve?

Fortunately, it is not necessary to cure the party addiction of Congress to start Project Athena. A group of private citizens devoted to the American Revolution, or a corporation or university wishing to lead in deliberation science, or even a billionaire fed up with our moral and political ignorance, could start the Project that will make the dangerous vice of party politics passé, and Congress itself irrelevant.  The time is surely ripe to bring our republic into the twenty-first century; the competition from even a single private initiative would certainly get the attention of the President, the Congress, and the Supreme Court.  It might even reform them.

**Thomas Jefferson:** "Life is of no value but as it brings us gratifications.  Among the most valuable of these is rational society.  It informs the mind, sweetens the temper, chears our spirits, and promotes health."

Jefferson believed that in Europe the Age of Reason was produced through the influence of science.  He wanted that same influence to bring about the Age of Common Reason, that would transform America into a "rational society."  Today that requires the thorough integration of intelligence mechanized by computers and humanized by courts of common reason.  Isn't it incongruous that we spend vast sums improving the artificial intelligence of computers, but decline to spend similar sums improving the natural intelligence of humans, although they display the most individual and collaborative intelligence of anything in the universe that we know of?  Project Athena would spend those similar sums by experimenting with the design and administration of juries in order to surpass human individual intelligence operating at its best.  By uniting that effort with contemporary artificial intelligence, Project Athena might produce an entirely new *democratic superintelligence* that matches language or the computer in its importance for the ascent of humanity.  Wouldn't it be an interesting experiment to pit a jury of our 535 legislators against a jury of citizens consisting of

535 subjuries to see which has the greater deliberative competence? Even if Dual Freedoms Courts uniting ethics, economics, and politics prove to be unachievable, Athena might nevertheless be better than our legislatures at ameliorating the calamities that America now faces. Consider the crudity and dangers of people having to take to the streets to express their moral grievances, such as was done over the Vietnam war, Jim Crow, Occupy Wall Street, and Black Lives Matter. Parties have been the principal system in "systemic racism, " they are structured to obstruct moral progress.

**John Adams:** "No sooner has one Party discovered or invented an Amelioration of the Condition of Man or the order of Society, than the opposite Party, belies it, misconstrues it, misrepresents it, ridicules it, insults it, and persecutes it."

Addiction to drink or cigarettes or gambling brings great pleasure when one gets the alcohol or nicotine or a win. That pleasure is dangerous to the individual. Those who have a vulnerability to revenge addiction are attracted to party politics because there they can get back at perceived enemies. That addiction is dangerous to the country. "Power is the ultimate aphrodisiac," says Henry Kissinger. Historically, the intransigence of one party or the other has undermined attempts at real advances in racial harmony. The only way parties can redeem themselves is to pass legislation that creates a "rational society" with institutional structures that are safe, subtle, and so effective in correcting grievances and promoting public happiness as to make parties and going to the streets forever extinct.

If Project Athena were successful, the people, when they are ready, could write their own Constitution that "inspires them with a conscious dignity, becoming Freemen." Long experience with courts of common reason would allow the new constitution to be the most carefully composed document in human history, perhaps by using higher standards of excellence than we today can even conceive. But we can imagine that, like fundamental science, the document would be beautiful. Two of the most important innovators in quantum mechanics were Paul Dirac and Erwin Schrödinger. Dirac wrote to Schrödinger that they "had a very strong appreciation of mathematical beauty" which "was like a religion with us. It was a very profitable religion to hold, and can be considered as the basis of much of our success." The successes of the Declaration and the Constitution were a product of the very profitable civic religion that aspires to political beauty and perfection. The pithy and awesome rhetoric of the Declaration was an essential part of its greatness; so was the language of the Constitution:

**Fisher Ames (1788):** "Considered merely as a literary performance, [the Constitution] was an honour to our country."

The Constitution was then seen as an attempt to achieve a perfect government that would begin and continue to operate consistently in the cause of humanity. Here is the reasoning.

**James Madison:** "Each individual being previously independent of the others, the compact which is to make them one society must result from the free consent of *every* individual." (Madison used italics, I think, to emphasize the equal dignity and autonomy embedded in America's political philosophy.)

The Constitution—that is, the American compact—must be interpreted as being agreed to by "*every* individual," which requires that "WE THE PEOPLE OF THE UNITED STATES," refers to all those under its jurisdiction, very much including women, blacks, white slaves, and native Americans. (The same reasoning would apply to Virginia if the union of the states is considered a mere confederacy.) Therefore "every individual" must be recognized in constitutions by interpreting each provision so that it would be reasonable for them voluntarily to accept the compact. For instance, English is ambiguous. "He" can mean *male*, or alternatively, *male or female*. The latter sense must be chosen when the Constitution uses "he" to refer to the President. Furthermore, the Constitution says: "No Person held to Service or Labour in one State, under the Laws thereof, escaping into another, shall, in Consequence of any Law or Regulation therein, be discharged from such Service or Labour, but shall be delivered up on Claim of the Party to whom such Service or Labour may be due." This might refer to an indentured servant that is trying to abdicate responsibility to fulfill a legitimate contract. But by the philosophy of the American Revolution it cannot refer to slaves, for that philosophy requires revolt against tyrants, even petty ones, for tyrants are all natural law criminals.

**Thomas Jefferson:** "Rebellion to Tyrants is Obedience to God."

**Declaration of Independence:** "But when a long train of abuses and usurpations, pursuing invariably the same Object evinces a design to reduce them under absolute Despotism, it is their right, it is their Duty, to throw off such Government." (Frederick Douglass: "If [a slave] kills his master, he imitates only the heroes of the revolution.")

**John Hancock (July 5, 1776):** John Hancock writing to the New Jersey Convention, enclosed the Declaration "in Obedience to the Command of Congress," and spoke of the "important Consequences resulting to the American States from this Declaration of Independence, considered as the Ground & Foundation of a future Government."

Hence it became common to date political events by their yearly distance from the Declaration. The Articles of Confederation states it is "in the third year," the journal of the Constitutional Convention begins by saying it is in the "eleventh year," the Constitution itself ends by saying it is in the "Twelfth" year, the first use of the Great Seal of the United States was in the "fourteenth," year, the conclusion of the document creating the capital of the United States was in the "fifteenth" year.

Hancock's prescience that the Declaration would serve "as the Ground & Foundation of a future Government" is found in the Ninth Amendment: 'The enumeration in the Constitution of certain rights, shall not be construed to deny or disparage others retained by the people." It is self-evident that the rights retained by the people must include the Declaration's "unalienable Rights" of "Life, Liberty, and the pursuit of Happiness." The Declaration and Constitution were made for each other (in the same room) during the "Twelfth" year, and they consummated their union in the sixteenth year with the adoption of the Bill of Rights.

By the philosophy of the American revolution, the Constitution must be interpreted in the cause of humanity. That philosophy was inspired by Cicero and by Edward Coke, the greatest Elizabethan jurist. Cicero: "In the very definition of the term 'law' there inheres the idea and principle of choosing what is just and true." Coke: "When the construction of any act is left to the law, the law, which abhorreth injury and wrong will never so construe it, as shall work a wrong." "*Nota*, the rehearsal or preamble of the statute is a good mean to find out the meaning of the statute, and as it were a key to open the understanding thereof." "How long soever it hath continued, if it be against reason it is of no force in law." These principles make proslavery interpretations of the American Constitution void: First, they are not "just and true." Second, they do not "abhorreth injury"; Third, they are incompatible with the Preamble which begins: "WE THE PEOPLE OF THE UNITED STATES, in Order to form a more perfect Union, establish Justice." Fourth, the long existence of hereditary slavery in the United States has no legal weight whatsoever. Now consider some American voices advocating humane rules of interpretation:

**James Otis (1764):** "Should an act of parliament be against any of [*God's*] natural laws, which are *immutably* true, *their* declaration would be contrary to eternal truth, equity and justice, and consequently void."

**George Clinton:** "When laws are made, not contradictory to the letter of the constitution, but repugnant to the general good, the constitution is violated; because the general good is the foundation of the social compact."

**Benjamin Rush (1786):** "Nothing can be politically right, that is morally wrong; and no necessity can ever sanctify a law, that is contrary to equity. Virtue is the living principle of a republic." (Remember, the Constitution, says the "United States shall guarantee to every state in this union a Republican form of government," which makes it into an explicit antislavery document. Further, the speech of Douglass — "The Meaning of July Fourth for the Negro"(1852) — should be ranked in importance with the Gettysburg Address and they should always be studied as a pair. Yet their major theme can be summed up in Rush's first nine words.)

By humane rules of interpretation, the rule of law requires that any apparent law — even if it be a clause in the Constitution — for which there is no reasonable interpretation that does not cause injury, is not law. Hence the necessity of a bill of rights to define the meaning of "injury" so that American governments nowhere impede, and everywhere encourage, the pursuit of a flourishing life.

**Thomas Jefferson:** "A bill of rights is what the people are entitled to against every government on earth, general or particular, and what no just government should refuse, or rest on inference."

This expresses an important part of America's revolutionary philosophy. Unfortunately, as is frequently the case with Jefferson, his devotion to the principles he expresses is questionable. Hence, in 1792, when it was Jefferson's duty as Secretary of State to officially inform the states of the successful passage of the Bill of Rights, we might expect that he would use this occasion to write a magnificent letter with soaring rhetoric celebrating this glorious achievement as of the highest importance not only for Americans, but for all humanity. Had he done so, it is likely the letter would rival even the Declaration in the fame that posterity could rightly bestow upon it. Yet such a letter would also call attention to the contradiction between the Bill of Rights and the existence of slavery in the United States. It was Jefferson's moral cowardice that prevented him from facing that contradiction, whether in his private life or his public career. If his Declaration of American Racism was an inordinate sin of commission against the cause of humanity, the following letter, quoted in full, is an inordinate sin of omission. It treats the Bill of Rights as an afterthought, which was then followed, in the same aristocratic spirit, by a Supreme Court which then took more than a century and a half to discover that the Bill of Rights was not written in invisible ink.

To the Governors of the several States.
Philadelphia March 1 1792.

Sir

I have the honor to send you herein enclosed, two copies duly authenticated, of an Act concerning certain fisheries of the United States, and for the regulation and government of the fishermen employed therein; also of an Act to establish the post office and post roads within the United States; also the ratifications, by three fourths of the Legislatures of the several States, of certain articles in addition to and amendment of the Constitution of the United States, proposed by Congress to the said Legislatures, and of being with sentiments of the most perfect respect, your Excellency's &.

Th: Jefferson

"Hypocrisy," declares La Rochefoucauld's fine epigram, "is the homage that vice pays to virtue." This observation applies equally well to the "internal hypocrisy" of self-deceit when thinking about one's own probity. If hypocrisy and self-deceit concerning slavery and race allowed the Founders to compose a Constitution and Bill of Rights appropriate for a free people, and then they give their composition a racist interpretation that protects slavery, why should those free of that hypocrisy and self-deceit, be obligated to find it there? They aren't. Frederick Douglass, certainly free of proslavery sentiments and racist prejudice against blacks, rightly believed the Constitution to be a "GLORIOUS LIBERTY DOCUMENT" that created an "anti-slavery government."

**Virginia Declaration of Rights (June 12, 1776):** George Mason said that "of all the various modes and forms of Government, that is best which is capable of producing the greatest degree of happiness and safety, and is most effectually secured against the danger of mal-administration."

From the beginning the members of the Supreme Court

violated humane rules of legal interpretation — maladministration of the highest order — so they could justify slavery as legal. The fault was not in the Constitution or the stars, but in the moral character of those that tolerated, practiced, and expanded an American Holocaust, while often thinking of themselves, like Madison did, as having "a uniform zeal for a republican government." And thus it is ironic and lamentable that so often in middle schools and high schools, in colleges and universities, in scholarly articles and news media of all types, that we are exhorted to seize the "moral high ground" and interpret the Constitution as proslavery, *a claim that implicitly rejects the humane rules of interpretation required by the philosophical theory on which the Constitution is based.*

Historically, a corruption of consciousness was necessary to "legally" allow hereditary slavery until the Civil War, then hereditary re-enslavement (peonage) until World War II, and finally hereditary Jim Crow until the 1960s. Why emulate this gross moral catastrophe of proslavery interpretation that commonly required self-deceit to make it tolerable for the perpetrators to live with themselves? Fighting such horrors as racism and slavery is admirable, and claims of the "moral high ground" need not always be wrong, but such claims must be backed by honest, hard, and often tedious work of historical and philosophical analysis, in order to survey exactly where that "moral high ground" can be found. This effort would require facing many questions, such as: How do I refute the same arguments that nevertheless convinced Douglass to change his mind (1851) and henceforth understand the Constitution to be antislavery? Slavery, he claimed *"never was lawful, and never can be made so."* Again, If I were on the Supreme Court when the Dred Scott case (1857) came before me, would I have contradicted Douglass and instead bonded with Chief Justice Taney in grossly violating humane rules of interpretation in order to find racial slavery — and its expansion — as legally protected by the Constitution? Would I have joined Taney in thinking the decision was creating a more perfect union? What becomes of my moral integrity if I would have proclaimed an antislavery Constitution in 1857, and a proslavery Constitution today?

Nevertheless, all the Constitution's eighteenth-century virtues are not, in the twenty-first century, supporting a secure and flourishing life for every American. We know what we must do:

**James Madison:** "As the people are the only legitimate fountain of power, and it is from them that the constitutional charter, under which the several branches of government hold their power, is derived; it seems strictly consonant to the republican theory, to recur to the same original authority . . . whenever it may be necessary to . . . new-model the powers of government."

## A NEW AND JURiED CONSTITUTION

**Alexander Hamilton: From the** opening paragraphs of the *Federalist*: "It has been frequently remarked, that it seems to have been reserved to the people of this country, by their conduct and example, to decide the important question, whether societies of men are really capable or not, of establishing good government from reflection and choice, or whether they are forever destined to depend, for their political constitutions, on accident and force. If there be any truth in the remark, the crisis, at which we are arrived, may with propriety be regarded as the æra in which that decision is to be made; and a wrong election of the part we shall act, may, in this view, deserve to be considered as the general misfortune of mankind. This idea will add the inducements of philanthropy to those of patriotism to heighten the solicitude, which all considerate and good men must feel for the event."

Project Athena would not only require that the present Constitution be read with humane principles of interpretation, it would eventually oversee the adaption of a new, juried Constitution that would be a perfect reflection of the wisdom and philanthropy of the American people,

**James Madison:** In the speech in which Madison introduced what became the Bill of Rights he argued "That there be prefixed to the constitution a declaration—That all power is originally vested in, and consequently derived from the people. That government is instituted, and ought to be exercised for the benefit of the people; which consists in the enjoyment of life and liberty, with the right of acquiring and using property, and generally of pursuing and obtaining happiness and safety. That the people have an indubitable, unalienable, and indefeasible right to reform or change their government, whenever it be found adverse or inadequate to the purposes of its institution." (Thus the Declaration and Constitution were intended to be mutually supportive by the "Father" of both the Constitution and the Bill of Rights.)

Our new Constitution would follow the spirit of Madison's suggestion by having its initial section state the ethical and political axioms of the American Revolution, which might include parts of the Declaration, Rush's nine words, the entire Preamble, excerpts from Lincoln's writings, and inspiring phrases from other political writing since then. It would also state that it must be interpreted humanely. The second section would be a bill of rights.

**James Wilson:** "To every suggestion concerning a bill of rights, the citizens of the United States may always say, WE reserve the right to do what we please."

Courts of Common Reason would determine what rights actually "please" the people. These rights would generate the rules that must be followed for the government to play the game of Dignity correctly. The third section would lay down the branches of the government: Executive, Legislative, Judicial, and Deliberative. The latter would transform the Agency for Common Reason into a branch of government. Its function would be to reflect the cognitive, emotional, and volitional aspects of the American people with the least possible distortion. It would be the Bell Labs of America's juried democracy. That would necessitate constant attention to the identification and maintenance of the axioms of the American Revolution that Mason and Wilson spoke of at the opening of this book. Metajuries would decide how these principles would be incorporated into the operation of all Courts of Common Reason.

A special Festival America for the new Constitution would commemorate its introduction in song, dance, theater, music, and ritual. The initial section expressing the philosophy of the American Revolution would be poetic, impassioned, and composed with magisterial concision, in order to inspire great awe, so that philosophy would never be forgotten again, even for a day. It could be set to music, incorporated into a new national anthem with parts of it used in a new pledge of allegiance to the American people; the aim would be a perfect union of political philosophy and political art. It should be eloquent when read, stirring when sung, and use a natural flow of ideas and rhyme to ease memorization by students in primary and secondary schools. What is learned by heart is taken to heart; an intense yearning for excellence in personal and public self-government should be instilled so that children identify themselves with the aspirational basis of American civilization. Aristotle's comment is relevant: "The best laws, though sanctioned by every citizen of the state, will be of no avail unless the young are trained by habit and education in the spirit of the constitution." That educational effort is necessary to demonstrate that the American people do not have a special place within the American Revolution, their lives *are* the American Revolution; their pursuit of happiness and the flourishing of all humanity is its quintessence.

**James Wilson:** "Is a toast asked? 'The *United States*,' instead of the 'People of the *United States*,' is the toast given. This is not politically correct. The toast is meant to present to view the *first* great object in the *Union*: It presents only the second: It presents only the *artificial* person, instead of the *natural* persons, who spoke it into existence." "A *State*; useful and valuable as the contrivance is, is the *inferior* contrivance of *man*; and from his *native* dignity derives all its *acquired* importance."

**David Ramsay:** "The far famed social compact between the people and their rulers, did not apply to the United States. The sovereignty was in the people."

To emphasize the people's "*native* dignity" and "sovereignty" the new Constitution would have no *official* written copy. Rather, it would reintroduce the oral tradition of our preliterate ancestors and have the only *official* version be preserved, not in argon gas, but in the collective memory of the American people "who spoke it into existence." It would then be clear, as it now is unfortunately not, that the people give the Constitution the only life it has, that any authoritative understanding of its text must finally rest in their minds, hearts, and wills. Henceforth our toasts would all become, in Wilson's sense, "politically correct" because the awe that patriots feel toward the new Constitution would not be to parchment under glass, but to the sublime spirit of the American people in its finest political expression, a spirit that protects and celebrates our individuality, our freedoms, and our pursuits of happiness.

Given the way the new Constitution was created and preserved, given its frequent communal expression, given the extraordinary capacity for spectacle that contemporary technology has made possible, the new government would inevitably have the fervent and rational support of the citizens of the United States, because they authorized it to be the supreme embodiment of their common humanity. What we owe the next generation is a truly excellent twenty-first-century, juried democracy, combined with an education that would write on their minds, hearts, and wills the ethical, economic, political, and aspirational virtues that they will need to produce flourishing and emotionally rewarding lives for themselves and their country.

In a remarkable letter written to Gouverneur Morris on February 29, 1802, Hamilton confesses: "Mine is an odd destiny. Perhaps no man in the UStates has sacrificed or done more for the present Constitution than myself—and contrary to all my anticipations of its fate, as you know from the very beginning I am still labouring to prop the frail and worthless fabric. [During the Constitutional Convention Hamilton "acknowledged himself not to think favorably of Republican Government."] Yet I have the murmurs of its friends no less than the curses of its foes for my rewards. What can I do better than withdraw from the Scene? Every day proves to me more and more that this American world was not made for me."

Had the composer of the last sentence been unknown to me, and I was asked to guess its provenance, I would have said a student or faculty radical, in a moment of despair, at an American college or university in the 1960s, or after the 2016 election. Hamilton's alienation could hardly be more poignantly expressed, yet he did not abandon his country.  Indeed fifteen years after the signing of the American Constitution—and just twenty days after he wrote the letter—Hamilton articulated how a new constitution could be created that would not be a "frail and worthless fabric."

**Alexander Hamilton:** "A people, who sacrificing their prejudices on the altar of experience, and spurning the artifices of insidious Demagogues, could, as a deliberate act of national reason, adopt and establish for themselves a Constitution which bid fair to immortalize their glory and their happiness."

Today we rightly honor this immigrant as never before, by reading Ron Chernow's superb biography, and by enjoying the poetry, songs, and dance of Lin-Manuel Miranda's remarkable musical.  But Hamilton's vision continues to be so unknown that even our most patriotic and imaginative leaders do not advocate establishing institutions that would make such "a deliberate act of national reason" possible.  After more than two centuries, Hamilton's magnificent vision remains but an idle American dream.

## HUMAN NATURE

And yet, of all the problems that might make humanity extinct, bad governments, especially among the major powers, stand in the way of solving any of the others.  America as an ideal is the greatest of the dreams of reason since it defines an environment in which reason's other dreams may be achieved.  But is it merely an idle dream?  Can dignity and moral law have more than the skeptic's game-theoretic reality?  This issue has a counterpart in the philosophy of mathematics. Consider the testimony of three mathematical giants.  G. H. Hardy writes that "317 is a prime, not because we think so, or because our minds are shaped in one way rather than another, but *because it is so*, because mathematical reality is built that way." Kurt Gödel thought "the objects and theorems of mathematics are as objective and independent of our free choice and our creative acts as is the physical world." Stephen Kleene claims that "if we are not to adopt a mathematical nihilism," then some mathematics must be more than a mere symbol game. Hence the true mathematical statement *There exists a prime number between 314 and 330* asserts a numerical existence independent of us. The eighteenth-century American revolutionists thought dignity had the same kind of *real, but abstract existence* that Hardy, Gödel, and Kleene assert for natural numbers. Like Tag, mathematics and politics are games, but, unlike Tag's mere game-created reality, their play is grounded in a *reality independent of the games*. To avoid "mathematical nihilism," some abstract properties, such as being prime, and some abstract entities, such as natural numbers, must have a supernatural existence to form the basis of natural science; to avoid political nihilism, some moral properties, such as dignity, and some moral entities, such as rights, must have a supernatural existence to form the basis of political science.

Nevertheless mathematics can be worth pursuing even if it has only a game-theoretic existence, with no further Pythagorean significance. The same is true for life itself.

**John Adams:** "A death bed, it is said, shews the emptiness of titles. That may be. But does it not equally shew the futility of riches, power, liberty, and all earthly things? The cloud-capt towers, the gorgeous palaces, the solemn temples, the great globe itself, appear the baseless fabric of a vision, and life itself a tale, told by an idiot, full of sound and fury, signifying nothing. Shall it be inferred from this, that fame, liberty, property, and life, shall be always despised and neglected? Shall laws and government, which regulate sublunary things be neglected, because they appear baubles at the hour of death?"

Adams means, I think, that even if our earthly existence has no cosmic significance, even then it is worth bothering about "fame, liberty, property, and life." Translation into contemporary terms: Even if the universe is meaningless, and humanity itself the accidental byproduct of a ghastly, evolutionary slaughterhouse, destined to end utterly devoid of any significance in a cosmic nanosecond, even then, the American Revolution is worth pursuing.

Whether or not it is justifiable for some games to have a Pythagorean existence, games do allow us to go validly from *is* to *ought*. If this is a game of chess, and if each player *is* trying to win, then, say, one player *ought* to make three moves to achieve checkmate. From a set of facts (*"is"*) a set of injunctions (*"ought"*) follows. "Games combining chance and skill give the best representation of human life"(Leibniz). According to American revolutionary politics, each player in the existential game of Dignity is trying to win (that is, pursuing happiness successfully), but may not use any means to win. Rather, each must play with an exemplary level of sportsmanship. Then, as in chess, certain oughts follow. "The city is best governed which has the greatest opportunity of obtaining happiness"(Aristotle). Consequently, in their revolutionary civic sports, Americans ought to produce "magical" governments that continually transcend any achieved level of "obtaining happiness."

**James Wilson:** "It is the glorious destiny of man to be always progressive."

**Thomas Jefferson:** "Questions of natural right are triable by their conformity with the moral sense and reason of man." "The principles on which we engaged, of which the charter of our independence is the record, were sanctioned by the laws of our being."

The evidence that there is a universal human nature has now been explosively enlarged, most spectacularly in the articulation of the human genome. What oughts are built into human nature? To answer that question, we need a science of deliberation to add to our knowledge of biology and the rest of the liberal arts and sciences. The ultimate aim is, as it were, to articulate the moral genome of human beings so that, as far as possible, the ignorance of ourselves would progressively be reduced. Such a genome, like its biological counterpart, is grounded in history, and is not fixed. It does not presuppose that humans are all exactly alike morally or politically, any more than a biological genome presupposes that we are all clones with no biochemical individuality. Yet its articulation would allow us to better determine the customs and laws that not only best fit human nature, but best fit the American character at this particular time.

**James Wilson:** "'Know thou thyself,' is an inscription peculiarly proper for the porch of the temple of science. The knowledge of human nature is of all human knowledge the most curious and the most important."

This view of science survives in our time. Thus Schrödinger states that the "scope, aim and value" of science "is the same as that of any other branch of human knowledge. Nay, none of them alone, only the union of all of them, has any scope or value at all, and that is simply enough described: it is to obey the command of the Delphic deity, Γνῶθι σεαυτόν, get to know yourself." America is a kind of research program to test experimentally the proposition that the vocation of humankind is to recognize that we are jointly playing a game by living, whose point is to so organize ourselves that we may use reason to discover the laws of our nature, the ideals of an excellent life, and the habits necessary or desirable to pursue that life. The American Revolution is an Enlightenment game changer.

In order to determine what, if any, aspirational political principles are built into human nature, Project Athena would test whether those of the United States match the principles articulated at other times and places, especially where they are independently produced. Perhaps the most remarkable evidence of such American cosmopolitanism comes from the expressions used by Lipit-Ishtar in ancient Sumer, and by Gouverneur Morris in revolutionary America, when composing a proper introduction to fundamental law. The space-time divide could hardly be greater, yet they are uncannily similar. The parallels were first pointed out in 1994 by James T. McGuire. (Anu is the god of the sky, while Enlil is the god of kingship and the king of the gods. The Sumer text is fragmented.)

| Sumer, circa 1900 B.C. | United States, 1787. |
|---|---|
| **The Law Code of Lipit-Ishtar** | **The Federal Constitution** |

| **Prologue** | **Preamble** |
|---|---|
| . . . when Anu (and) Enlil had called Lipit-Ishtar . . . to the princeship of the land | WE THE PEOPLE OF THE UNITED STATES, |
| in order to | in Order to form a more perfect Union, |
| establish justice in the land, | establish Justice, |
| to banish complaints, | insure domestic Tranquility, |
| to turn back enmity and rebellion by the force of arms, | provide for the common defence, |
| (and) to bring well-being to the Sumerians and Akkadians, | promote the general Welfare, |
| then I, Lipit-Ishtar . . . [estab]lished [jus]tice in [Su]mer and Akkad in accordance with the word of Enlil. | and secure the Blessings of Liberty to ourselves and our Posterity, do ordain and establish this Constitution for |

Verily, in those [days] I *procured . . .* the United States of America.
the [fre]edom of the [so]ns and
daughters of [Nippur], the [so]ns and
daughters of Ur, the sons and
daughters of [I]sin, the [so]ns and
daughters of [Sum]er (and) Akkad
*upon whom . . .* slaveship *. . . had*
*been imposed.*

**John Jay:** Jay said the Preamble's purposes "collectively comprise every thing requisite, with the blessings of Divine Providence, to render a people prosperous and happy."

It certainly seems likely that Lipit-Ishtar would have said something similar about his Prologue. Lipit-Ishtar lived a thousand years before Homer, whose *Iliad* marks the beginning of the West, and 3,600 years before our Constitution was composed by delegates who could not have known of Sumer's existence. Perhaps John Adams was right when he said that there "is no special providence for Americans, and their nature is the same with that of others."

**Thomas Paine (January 1776):** "The cause of America is in a great measure the cause of all mankind."

**Benjamin Franklin (1777):** Writing from Paris Franklin said: " 'Tis a Common Observation here that our Cause is *the Cause of all Mankind*; and that we are fighting for their Liberty in defending our own. 'Tis a glorious task assign'd us by Providence; which has I trust given us Spirit and Virtue equal to it, and will at last crown it with Success."

**George Washington (1779):** "Our cause is noble, it is the cause of Mankind!"

**Gouverneur Morris (1779):** The following quotation comes from a booklet that was "published according to a resolution of Congress": "The portals of the temple we have raised to freedom, shall . . . be thrown wide, as an asylum to mankind. America shall receive to her bosom and comfort and cheer the oppressed, the miserable and the poor of every nation and of every clime. . . . In becoming acquainted with the religions, the customs and the laws, the wisdom, virtues and follies and prejudices of different countries, we shall be taught to cherish the principles of general benevolence. We shall learn to consider all men as our brethren, being equally children of the Universal Parent - - - that God of the heavens and the earth."

Thus eight years before the Constitution, it was the understanding, that America, if it lived according to its ideals, was to have a cosmopolitan attraction, and destined to be made up of individuals coming from all cultures ("every nation") and all races ("every clime"). America was to be first in the cause of humanity. Its cosmopolitanism presupposes that all humans should be treated with equal dignity and equal justice, but our elective governments have often grossly violated those standards. Again, we may look to the Athenians for insight. The general lesson of *Eumenides* by Aeschylus is that blood vengeance is a systemic moral failure, that Athenian justice requires Athenian juries, since it is improper for even the goddess Athena to judge questions of murder. Like blood vengeance, elective democracy has proven itself to be a systemic moral failure. It is only American juries organized in Courts of Common Reason that should have ultimate political power; for example, only they should determine the operational meaning of property rights (such as free markets, eminent domain, or intellectual ownership) and property in rights (such as equality, liberty, or justice). In a decade, Project Athena has a fair chance of permanently correcting *systemic* moral failures and, in the meantime, of becoming a source of universal hope for all humanity.

American perfectionist democracy is not founded on the cosmopolitan ideals of a universal civilization in the abstract sense that is often found among intellectuals ("I rise above the parochial *hoi polloi* and refuse to be attached to any place or country."). Such attitudes might jeopardize legitimate personal, familial, cultural, or regional loyalties of a diverse citizenry; or it might even suggest the falsehood that omnipresent recognition of the dignity of individuals, or peoples, can be achieved by ignoring place, biography, voluntary associations, and history. Rather, American perfectionist democracy is based on universal, aspirational ideals as humanized by the common reason, decency, loves, and nobility of the American people, qualities that would be disclosed in their soul-searching deliberations to secure the blessings of liberty to themselves and their posterity. But if this humanization should ever result in moral breakdowns, then the remedy is Festival America, where artists can expose these failures, and so mortify and shame the people that they reform their values, manners, and character. And if these attempts continually miscarry, let it be rightly said that the American Revolution has, to that degree, failed.

## PROSPECTS

**Thomas Paine:** "When it shall be said in any country in the world, my poor are happy; neither ignorance nor distress is to be found among them; my jails are empty of prisoners, my streets of beggars; the aged are not in want, the taxes are not oppressive; the rational world is my friend, because I am a friend of its happiness: when these things can be said, then may that country boast of its constitution and its government."

American civilization is in many, many ways the best in the

world, with colossal achievements that rightfully make Americans enormously grateful and proud. Nevertheless, patriots cannot read Paine's words without severe anguish, for by these revolutionary standards, even in the 246th year of our independence,we can't boast at all; we are embarrassingly reduced to regret, shame, and tears.

**James Wilson:** "A progressive state is necessary to the happiness and perfection of man. Whatever attainments are already reached, attainments still higher should be pursued. Let us, therefore, strive with noble emulation. Let us suppose we have done nothing, while any thing yet remains to be done. Let us, with fervent zeal, press forward, and make unceasing advances in every thing that can support, improve, refine, or embellish society."

America's aesthetic ideal of universal moral equality and equal justice results in a revolutionary society where perfect happiness is an asymptote that cannot be reached, but which will be progressively approached by following curves whose equations are derived from the common reason of a free, liberally-educated people. America is seen as a great-souled country pursuing every civic excellence in the cause of humanity. This pursuit can rightly justify that national pride without which greatness is unlikely or impossible.

**Joel Barlow:** "One of the most operative means . . . of making mankind wiser and better than they are, is to convince them that they are capable of becoming so."

**James Wilson:** "To love and to deserve honest fame, is another duty of a people, as well as of an individual."

The aspirational perfectionism of the American Revolution is living, not graven; it requires that our laws or governments be changed whenever they no longer reflect the deliberate sense of living Americans. Whether it be an individual or a people, the truly great do not attempt to be best by the standards of their time; rather, they introduce new standards of excellence that others do not have enough intelligence, imagination, determination, passion, and opportunity to envisage and pursue. The members of the 1776 generation did this, they conceived a juried democracy in the cause of freedom, justice, and equality. If Project Athena were energetically pursued, America would certainly "deserve honest fame" among all lovers of humanity. But if, during that pursuit, some calamity put America to an end, Paine would surely speak for the lovers:

**Thomas Paine:** "It will not then be said, here stood a temple of vast antiquity; here rose a Babel of invisible height, or there a palace of sumptuous extravagance; but here, ah painful thought! the noblest work of human wisdom, the grandest scene of human glory, the fair cause of freedom rose and fell."

The United States began as an experiment to see if excellent self-government is possible. It is failing in the way the Hubble telescope initially failed. That first mirror distorted the stars, our initial political mirror (made up of elective representatives) distorts the American people. Project Athena aims to replace that mirror. On September 12, 1962, President Kennedy said that Project Apollo "will serve to organize and measure the best of our energies and skills; because that challenge is one that we're willing to accept; one we are unwilling to postpone, and one which we intend to win." That venturesome scientific and technological spirit must be applied to politics. Independence for the nation, no less than autonomy for the individual, requires honest and deliberative soul-searching, which now requires the risks of replacing a failing eighteenth-century mirror with a twenty-first-century one that precisely reflects the true humanity of the American people. A President who could persuade them to accept those risks by transforming America into a juried democracy, would be revolutionary in a sense that only Washington and Lincoln were; and if this example would spread to other countries, the President, like Pericles in Greece or Elizabeth in England, would rightly give a name to a new age, a global historical age establishing unprecedented economic, political, and moral prosperity. In evolutionary terms, humanity would finally finish the self-domestication of the species that has already been going on for thousands of years. All lovers of humanity would want to be in that number when this new world is revealed.

**Benjamin Franklin (1788):** "We are making Experiments in Politicks; What Knowledge we shall gain by them will be more certain, tho' perhaps we may hazard too much in that Mode of acquiring it."

When will we again be daring enough to "perhaps . . . hazard too much" by "making Experiments in Politicks," because Project Athena "is one that we are willing to accept, one we are unwilling to postpone, and one which we intend to win"? The American people must be persuaded to undertake the hazards of a great-souled political experiment that other countries would want to join and help perfect. American government should *earn* the continuing gratitude of a candid world by becoming first in the cause of humanity even, we may hope, first in the face of stiff competition.

**John Adams:** "Posterity! You will never know, how much it cost the present Generation, to preserve your Freedom! I hope you will make a good Use of it. If you do not I shall repent in Heaven, that I ever took half the Pains to preserve it."

Adams wanted America to know itself; we have done nothing to create institutions to achieve that goal. He wanted no political parties; we give them massive support. He wanted a "Representative Assembly" that is an "exact portrait of the people at large"; we have created no such thing, and our legislatures are highly unrepresentative in that sense. If he is judging us from heaven, he can only be repenting as he mutters "what fools these mortals be."

Adams claimed that the process by which the Constitution was realized to be "the greatest single effort of national deliberation that the world has ever seen." But suppose Project Athena were a magnificent success. Far from being embarrassed, as we are now, by ethical breakdowns, political stupidity, and philosophical ignorance, we could then have great delight in defending ourselves: "Forgive us, Mr. Adams. Your generation, with its Declaration, Constitution, and Bill of Rights, showed that you aspired to the highest degree of political excellence that was then possible. You did not have to create an American Revolution; you could have been satisfied with an American rebellion. You did not have to create the Constitution of 1787 or the Bill of Rights of 1991; you could have been satisfied to tinker with the Articles of Confederation. We, too, could have been satisfied with the fundamental political documents and institutions that we inherited from you and subsequent generations. Yet it was the striving for political excellence exemplified by your generation that inspired us to create, in contemporary America, a new perfection in government of, by, and for the people. As a result we have continued your revolution by revising the magnificent documents and institutions you have bequeathed to us. We have used standards of excellence that were impossible to achieve, or even imagine, in your age and have thus far exceeded the effort of national deliberation represented by the creation and adoption of the Constitution of 1787. So you need not repent in heaven, for our achievements demonstrate that we have made good use of the freedoms your generation created and our generation greatly enlarged, and that success was only possible because your example and philosophical dream inspired us to achieve it."

## BIBLIOGRAPHIC AND BIOGRAPHICAL REFERENCE

This book is meant to be a more accessible version of my *In the Cause of Humanity*. To achieve that goal, I have greatly shortened it, and eliminated a table of contents, bibliography, and index. Many of my words above have been taken without quotation marks from that book, sometimes exactly, sometimes revised. Almost all of the sources for the other quotations can be found there. They can also be checked on the Internet. Everywhere I tried to be as brief and clear as my talent and the subject matter allows.

Steve Courtney, my wife Shirley, and my son David read the manuscript. David also designed the wonderful cover. They all have my gratitude since, as a result, the book became significantly better.

I received a B.A. in Mathematics from Williams College (1957), and a Ph.D. in Philosophy from Princeton University (1960). I taught philosophy at Trinity College (Hartford, Connecticut) from 1960 until my retirement in 1999. I am the author of *A Profile of Mathematical Logic* (1970, 2004) and *In the Cause of Humanity* (2015, first edition 2010)

Edward Lorenz described the chaotic nature of the weather with a striking question: "*Does the Flap of a Butterfly's Wings in Brazil Set off a Tornado in Texas?*" Technically speaking, chaos is a kind of mean between complete randomness and complete order. There is order, but the road to the present will have had necessary elements of disorder. Human biography and history are likewise chaotic. A man gets a flat tire because of a nail. There is a nearby garage. While it is getting fixed he eats at a diner across the street and ends up marrying his waitress. I lack the talent of Tom Paine but, even so, for over fifty years, what kept me going was the infinitesimal chance that I could be a tiny butterfly that reawakens the mighty American revolution in this country I love so much.